Herbert P. Thomas

The Church and the Land

Being an Account of Inquiries into the Condition of some of the beneficed

Elergy

Herbert P. Thomas

The Church and the Land
Being an Account of Inquiries into the Condition of some of the beneficed Elergy

ISBN/EAN: 9783337063863

Printed in Europe, USA, Canada, Australia, Japan

Cover: Foto ©Lupo / pixelio.de

More available books at **www.hansebooks.com**

BEING AN ACCOUNT OF

INQUIRIES INTO THE CONDITION OF SOME OF THE BENEFICED CLERGY IN THE AUTUMN OF 1887

BY

HERBERT P. THOMAS

RIVINGTONS
WATERLOO PLACE, LONDON
MDCCCLXXXVII

PREFACE

IN the following pages are republished, with substantial additions, letters contributed to the *Morning Post* newspaper in September and October, 1887. I trust that they may at least supplement Mr. Prothero's admirable work, to which I am much indebted.

I have made three suggestions, which I venture to think deserve the consideration of those interested in Church legislation.

I. That tithes should be collected by the Ecclesiastical Commissioners (pp. 73, 104).

II. That in the case of all future appointments episcopal incomes should not be of fixed amount, but should vary with the tithe averages (p. 107); and

III. That the Ecclesiastical Commissioners should be empowered to make temporary grants to livings the value of which is temporarily depressed (p. 105).

I wish to draw particular attention to a letter printed in the Appendix, which shows the sort of straits to which many of the clergy in the Midlands are now reduced.

I have to express my obligations to the bishops, archdeacons, beneficed clergy, land agents, and others, who have furnished me with information, and from whom, without exception, I have received the most cordial assistance. It would not have been wonderful if some, at least, of those to whom I applied had resented the inquiries of a newspaper writer as to their income and their circumstances; but I met with no such case. I hope it will not seem ungrateful to many other informants if I mention the names of the Bishop Suffragan of Nottingham, the Archdeacons of Oakham and Nottingham, the Hon. E. P. Thesiger, C.B., Mr. Beadell, M.P., Mr. Aston, of the Queen Anne's Bounty Office, Mr. Porter, of the Ecclesiastical Commission, and last, but not least, the Rev. J. M. Dolphin, Vicar of Coddington, as those to whom I am particularly indebted. I ought, perhaps, to add that, although in individual instances I was authorized, without any restriction, to use the information given me, I thought it best to adhere to the uniform rule of not giving names, but only cases, since many of my correspondents stipulated that their poverty should not be published to the world. I may say, however, that I took some pains to secure accurate information, and that the particulars given are, in most instances, founded on duly authenticated statements now in my possession.

Finally, I have to thank the proprietors of the *Morning Post* for kindly allowing this republication.

CONTENTS

CHAPTER		PAGE
I.	Preliminary	1
II.	The Diocese of Southwell	11
III.	The Diocese of Lincoln	21
IV.	The Diocese of Ely	33
V.	The Diocese of Peterborough	42
VI.	Glebes generally	51
VII.	Tithes	61
VIII.	Tithes (*continued*)	71
IX.	Charges on Livings	86
X.	Recapitulation	97
	Appendix	111

CHAPTER I.

PRELIMINARY.

WHEN it was suggested that the best form in which the Church of England could celebrate the Jubilee was the erection of a Church House, a loud outcry arose from many quarters. Is it reasonable, people asked, to spend money on bricks and mortar at a time when the incomes of the clergy are lower than they have ever been before, when incumbents are resigning livings to take curacies, and when many, who a few years ago had a comfortable stipend, are now reduced to the brink of ruin? Would it not be much better to collect a relief fund for cases of clerical distress? Of course the answer was obvious. A subscription raised to commemorate a particular event must not be paid away without anything being left to show for it, or where is the memorial? Assuming that it had been possible to obtain £100,000 for the purpose, it would have been necessary, for this reason, to keep the capital intact; and the utmost that could be done would be to distribute the income of, say, £3000 a year, among the poor clergy. But this would be a mere drop in the ocean. The Ecclesiastical Commissioners themselves grant about £754,000 annually in augmentation of poor benefices, and £3000 more or less would make comparatively little difference. Then, the further objection was urged that though the clergy had doubtless suffered by the agricultural depression, they had fared no worse than the rest of the community; that they in some respects possessed special advantages, since commuted tithes were easier to collect than rent, and that it was quite wrong to infer from a few isolated cases that acute distress was general among them. Finally, it was decided to persevere with the scheme for the Church House, though the subscriptions no doubt fell off in consequence of the discussion, while an independent fund was raised for exceptional cases of distress among the clergy, this latter fund standing on its own merits, and not professing to be in any sense commemorative. It has been raised under the auspices of the Corporation of the Sons of the Clergy, the oldest and best known of clerical charities; and the fact that it has in the course of a few months reached something like £40,000, of which about half has already been distributed, shows that there is at any rate a widespread belief in the need for it.

It was to the extent and character of the clerical distress, to the questions how far it is likely to be of a lasting character, and what permanent remedies for it are likely to be found, that my inquiries were directed, and with this object I visited some of the dioceses most affected, and made some personal investigation of particular cases, having first received much valuable information from the Corporation of the Sons of the Clergy, already mentioned, from the offices of Queen Anne's Bounty and the Ecclesiastical Commission, from the Rent Guarantee Society, and from other sources.

It will be convenient, before detailing the results of those inquiries, that I should clear the way by the statement of some general facts, availing myself also for this purpose of the labours of Mr. R. E. Prothero, who has published in a collected form the admirable papers on the subject which he contributed to the *Guardian* newspaper. My only grudge against him is that he has, so to speak, taken the words out of my mouth as regards several of the questions on which I have to write, and I feel inclined to apply to him the old anathema, " Pereant qui ante nos nostra dixerint."

Speaking generally, the stipends of the beneficed clergy are derived either from tithe, from glebe, or from grants from the Ecclesiastical Commissioners. The last-named grants are of fixed amount, and are, therefore, individually unaffected by the land question, although the estates vested in the Commissioners have seriously fallen in value of late years, and they have, consequently, had to give notice that the field for new benefactions must be in future considerably restricted. But this does not apply to livings that have been already augmented, and the incumbents of such livings are comparatively fortunate. The case is different with the large class of rectors and vicars who are entirely, or almost entirely, dependent on tithe rent-charge. No doubt they or their predecessors have heretofore had little to complain of, for during the half-century which has elapsed since the commutation of tithes the charge has, on the whole, been slightly above par. It is calculated on the average prices of wheat, oats, and barley, during a period of seven years; and although on one or two occasions the prices of a particular year have been even lower than those of 1886, yet there has never before been such a succession of low prices as since 1880. Unfortunately, too, they show no signs of recovery. The tithe rent-charge, if it were reckoned on the prices of last year alone, would be only £75 1s. 7d. per cent. of the original commutation, whereas it is actually £87 8s. 10d. The level to which it is ultimately likely to sink is, in the opinion of good authorities, between £70 and £75. Even now the loss to many incumbents is terribly serious, especially as in a large number of cases they accepted their benefices when the tithe averages were high; for, a dozen years ago, parsons were like everybody else in supposing that landed property was absolutely certain to increase in value. Banks, it was said, might break, companies might collapse, stocks and shares might fall, but, with a steadily increasing population on a fixed area, it was impossible to believe that rents would go down. The land cannot be taken away or dissipated, and so people thought that its value must rise.

Of this notion landowners in general have been rudely disabused, and the clergy most of all. Here is an instance of what has happened in scores of cases. In 1875, a clergyman, with scarcely any private means, married on a living which was worth just £200 a year and a house, the tithe average being then nearly 13 above par. A family has now to be provided for; expenses of all kinds have increased; but the rent-charge has already fallen from £200 to £154, and in the course of five or six years more it is not unlikely to be as low as £140. But what business, some people will ask, has any gentleman to marry on even £200 a year? The answer is that popular feeling is against a celibate priesthood; that only a married man can without awkwardness perform some of the duties with which a clergyman is charged at the sick-bed and elsewhere in relation to the female members of his flock; that a parson's wife is almost as necessary as a parson in the organization of a parish ("I am the rector," said one of them, " but my wife is the director, and my daughter the mis-director"); and, finally, that, as Mark Twain has said, there is a good deal of human nature about most men. A charming little parsonage, embowered in roses and jessamine, with a wife who will, of course, be a perfect helpmate, and a trim little maidservant, who will be the most economical of her kind, is an ideal that infatuated curates may be forgiven for accepting as reality, with little thought of a probable family and of possible hard times. In fact, they have no alternative. Forty years ago there were less than six thousand beneficed clergymen. Now, owing to the abolition of pluralities, and the creation of new parishes, there are between thirteen and fourteen thousand incumbents; but even the nominal incomes of an overwhelming proportion are terribly small. Of the entire number of livings in England, more than one-third are worth less than £200 a year, considerably more than one-half are worth less than £300; and only about two thousand, or less than one-sixth of the whole, are of even the reputed value of £500 annually. Even assuming, therefore, that the livings were to be distributed with mathematical accuracy among all clergymen, whether possessing talents and interest or not, and assuming also that each man would remain a curate during half the term of an average clerical career, it has been calculated that only one in five would have a chance of a benefice worth

£500 a year, and less than one-half would have a chance of one worth £300. And as the average value of livings is so small, while there is a demand that they should be filled by married men of education and good social standing, it is inevitable that cases of acute hardship should arise when the incomes fall. The instance I have mentioned, however, was that of a vicar paid from tithe rent-charge, and whose losses arose solely from the diminution consequent on the fall in the price of corn. This diminution, as already stated, is at present only about 12 per cent. on the par value, though it is nearly 25 per cent. since the time when many of the clergy accepted their livings; and, consequently, the titheowners, though very hardly treated in several ways which I shall discuss hereafter, are not the worst sufferers. It is those incumbents of rural parishes who derive all or nearly all their income from glebe lands, whose lot is now the most pitiable. In large tracts of country in the Midlands, land that used to be eagerly competed for by tenants willing and anxious to take it at 40s. or 50s. an acre, is now either tenantless, with no offers to rent it at any price, or fetches some 10s. or 15s. an acre. The parson thus sees himself deprived, not of an eighth or a tenth, but of, perhaps, three-quarters of his entire income, and in some cases the charges in the way of mortgages and payments to Queen Anne's Bounty actually exceed the amount received. I do not hesitate to say that a large proportion of the incumbents in the rural parishes of the Midlands would be in the direst necessity unless they were possessed of private means. Many of them are now in absolute want.[1] I have come across a case in which a rector and his wife have actually less than £40 a year as their whole means of subsistence, though the living has in good times been worth over £300 a year; and in the course of my inquiries, I am sorry to say that I have found many other instances of the same kind, of which I shall give some particulars. Some of these incumbents are resigning their livings, and more would do so if it were not, in the first place, for the hope that better times may come, and, in the second place, for the fear that they may fail to obtain employment as curates. For although the stipends of curates[2] are, oddly enough, higher than they have ever been, and a man with a university degree, if young and unmarried, may command from £140 to £150 a year as soon as he is in priests' orders, a clergyman advanced in life finds it very difficult to obtain a curacy. An incumbent not unnaturally likes to have a curate who

[1] See letter signed "Country Rector," printed in Appendix A to this volume.

[2] According to an estimate founded on advertisements inserted by incumbents in the *Ecclesiastical Gazette*, the average stipend of a curate in 1853 was £79; in 1863, £97; in 1873, £129. In 1887 it is certainly considerably higher still.

will carry out his wishes and fall into his ways, whereas he fancies, not without reason, that an ex-rector who has ruled a parish of his own for twenty or thirty years is not likely to lend himself very readily to a subordinate position. The wife, too, is sometimes a difficulty, and this kind of promotion downwards is rarely satisfactory to either party. As a general rule, therefore, the incumbent struggles on, perhaps spending his own scanty means in that most hopeless and ruinous occupation, amateur farming; perhaps increasing his burdens by mortgaging his glebe in order to make it more attractive by better farm-buildings or improved drainage. In some instances, when livings are resigned, it is absolutely impossible to find incumbents for them.

I do not propose to deal in this place with the details of individual cases, but I may mention one living on which the charges exceed the receipts by about £150 a year, so that the incumbent, if somebody could be discovered willing to take the cure, would have to pay that sum for the honour and glory of his position; a second, which is similarly worth less than nothing, and has consequently been vacant for some years; a third, which has a very fine and expensive house, with excellent stabling and extensive gardens, while the net income is only just over £100 a year, a good deal of which is swallowed up in necessary repairs. If that particular living, once worth over £1000 a year, were to become vacant, nobody without considerable private means would be able to accept it. But most of the clergy in the districts in question remain at their posts, however large the proportion of their incomes which has been swept away; and the fact that so many squires have left, and the tenant-farmers are becoming less and less able to subscribe for local expenses, throws more and more pecuniary responsibility on the back of the unlucky parson. Then there is no doubt that in past times the incumbent has often been allowed to borrow money for the erection of houses much too large in proportion to the value of the living; and the interest on the mortgage and the instalments of the principal fall very heavily on the present occupant. Again, assessment committees have treated clergymen very badly, and there are cases in which the tithe rent-charge pays nearly a quarter of the entire rates of the parish, although the tithe itself could not, at most, be equivalent to more than one-tenth of the produce. On all these points I shall have something to say presently; it is enough now to indicate some of the chief hardships of which the clergy complain, or which, it would perhaps be more accurate to state, they for the most part suffer in silence.

CHAPTER II.

THE DIOCESE OF SOUTHWELL.

I HAVE already pointed out that the clergy who have suffered most from the hard times are those who have to depend mainly upon glebe for their income, while those who are owners of tithe have not, speaking generally, lost more, and in many cases have lost less, than other landowners. Those, again, whose glebe consists chiefly of heavy arable land, which costs much to cultivate, and which, at the present price of corn, scarcely repays cultivation even at a merely nominal rent, have been reduced to the greatest straits, while those holding rich pasture in some few instances obtain almost as much for it as in prosperous times. The parts of the country, therefore, in which there is the most glebe and, at the same time, the most clay land, would presumably be those in which the clergy are now worst off, and this presumption is quite borne out by the facts. Now, the degree in which clerical incomes are dependent on glebe varies very much in different localities. In the diocese of

Canterbury, for instance, each benefice has, on an average, only 11 acres of glebe; and in that of Rochester the average is only 5 acres. On the other hand, in the diocese of Southwell, the average is 69 acres; in that of Lincoln, 116 acres; and in that of Peterborough, no less than 129 acres. It may be said roughly that in the Midlands the bulk of clerical incomes is derived from glebe, while elsewhere it comes mainly from tithe rent-charge. The explanation is probably to be found in the fact that in the Midlands the old system of community of cultivation obtained until the beginning of the present century, and that under the Enclosure Acts, which first assigned the land to individual occupiers, it was the rule to provide for the maintenance of the benefice, not by the imposition of tithes, but by allotting to the incumbent one-tenth of the land. It follows, therefore, that the district where the clergy are suffering most at the present time is that which includes the heavy clays of Notts, Lincolnshire, and Northamptonshire; and I believe that something like two-thirds of the whole amount of the special distress fund already distributed by the Corporation of the Sons of the Clergy, has gone to the three dioceses of Peterborough, Lincoln, and Southwell.

For this reason it seemed desirable to make some local inquiries in those regions, and I began my investigations at Southwell. That diocese, it will be remembered, was recently formed at the instance of the late Bishop of Lincoln, who felt that his own was too large to be superintended by one man, and it comprises the whole of the counties of Nottingham and Derby. It was hard to believe, from external appearances at the time of my visit, that agriculture was not flourishing there. The wheat harvest of 1887 was in most places abundant, and though the oats had not done well in the drought, and the turnips were dried up, the barley was to the outward eye a splendid crop. The farm buildings are almost everywhere in excellent condition, and much money has evidently been spent on drainage. But wheat at thirty shillings a quarter does not pay for the cost of growing it in these heavy soils, and the explanation of the evidence of expenditure on farm buildings and drainage is that landlords have laid out money for those objects as a bait for tenants. On all hands the same story is heard, that farming in these parts cannot be made to answer at present prices, and that more farms are likely to be thrown up this year than at any previous time.

Near Southwell itself the clergy are comparatively lucky, for when the property of the old collegiate body was absorbed by the Ecclesiastical Commissioners, the livings were mostly endowed with fixed stipends, and it is therefore the Commissioners, and not the incumbents, who farm the land,

and who have now the worst of the bargain. The clergy who have suffered most are those in East Nottinghamshire, especially about Newark and in the Trent Valley generally. The Archdeacon of Nottingham, who has himself a living in that district, and whose official duties make him acquainted with the circumstances of the parishes throughout the county, and the Rev. J. M. Dolphin, Vicar of Coddington, near Newark, whose work as travelling secretary to the Society for the Propagation of the Gospel gives him a wide knowledge of the condition of the clergy in various parts of England, were both good enough to give me much valuable information on the subject, and I cannot help coming to the conclusion that, in a very large number of cases in that neighbourhood, the incumbents of what used to be flourishing livings have had the greater part of their incomes swept away; that many are only maintaining themselves out of their private means; and that some who have no such means are reduced to the sorest straits. In the Trent Valley, successive years of floods have impoverished the land, and have in many instances done serious damage to buildings, bridges, and fences, and on the top of these misfortunes has come the long drought of last summer, which has dried up the pastures and destroyed the root crops. The result is that farmers on all sides have been giving up their holdings, and that the only persons willing to take glebe are those who have nothing to lose, who starve the land, and from whom it is very difficult to get any rent.

The following instance is one of many. Ten years ago a certain living was worth about £500 a year, the glebe being let at 45*s.* an acre. But the tenant became insolvent, threw up his holding, and the rector had to pay compensation for unexhausted improvements to the creditors. For this purpose he was forced to borrow on his policy of life insurance. Failing to obtain another tenant, he tried to farm the glebe himself, and borrowed capital to stock it. The land was a strong clay, requiring much horse labour, so of course he lost money, and eventually he was glad to let it at 15*s.* an acre to a tenant who has only small means, and who may or may not be able to pay that rent with anything like regularity. He thus finds himself with his income reduced to about £160 a year, less the interest and instalments of the two loans which he was forced to contract, and which practically swallow up nearly the whole. He is only saved from absolute destitution by the possession of very small private funds, and is, in fact, reduced to great poverty, being moreover deprived of all means of making provision for his wife and family. Another benefice was worth over £200 a year, arising from glebe which now with difficulty fetches one-fifth of that rent. The incumbent has no other source of income, and is "passing poor on £40 a year," out of which he has to keep up his parsonage. He is a University man of considerable attainments, and continues to perform the services of the Church, and to labour assiduously among his parishioners for wages which an artisan would despise. Another living used to bring in £250, but money had to be borrowed, first for the payment of dilapidations left by a bankrupt predecessor, then for the improvement of farm buildings; and the upshot is that the charges actually exceed the receipts, that the benefice is now vacant, and that nobody can be found to accept what is worth considerably less than nothing. Another, producing £180, was charged a few years ago with £200 for damages inflicted on the glebe by the Trent floods; the rector had no means of meeting the outlay; the living was sequestered; and he was, in effect, ruined. Another, with about 200 acres of glebe, formerly worth £500 a year, now only produces £88; and another, with a glebe of 175 acres which used to be rented at £400, is now worth £60. Another, with about 700 acres of glebe, used to produce £1100 a year; but its value has fallen so low, and so large a sum had to be paid on the last vacancy for unexhausted improvements upon the land which the tenant threw up, that the presentation for some time went begging, as nobody without private means could afford to take it.

The fact that the normal value of most of the livings in the diocese is exceedingly small, makes the incumbents ill able to bear their present losses. Many would, no doubt, be augmented by the Ecclesiastical Commissioners, but the Commissioners' estates have themselves suffered seriously, and they have therefore had to withhold their grants for lack of funds, just when help is most wanted. The general reduction in rent in the Trent Valley is stated to average from 30 to 50 per cent. within the last ten years, and in individual cases the value of land is at present *nil*. Many landowners have suffered so severely that they have had to break up their establishments; and as neither squires nor farmers have any spare money, the main burden of supporting local institutions— schools and clothing clubs, dispensaries and sick funds—inevitably falls on the parsons. I heard of more than one instance in which all servants had been dismissed, and daughters had taken their places in discharging even the most menial household duties; but this necessity, though unpleasant, is probably not without some compensating advantages. Where the pinch of poverty is most felt is where school education has to be stopped; the premiums of insurances, by which it was hoped to make provision for wife and children, can no longer be paid; illness comes without the means of paying doctors' bills or of providing the luxuries which for a sick-room are necessities; and, worst of all, where the parson in his work amongst his parishioners is brought into contact with cases of acute distress, which he would fain relieve, as usual, with something more than words, but which he has now no power to help.

Many of these incumbents, too, have the unfortunate consciousness of having spent, on unsuccessful endeavours to farm their land, capital of their own which would, if otherwise invested, have been a permanent source of income, but which has, in fact, been absolutely swallowed up, without anything being left to show for it. It is no doubt very undesirable that a clergyman should turn farmer. The objections have been recognized by the Legislature, and an Act of 1838 prohibits any "spiritual person" from renting above eighty acres of land without the bishop's express permission, which is only to be given for a limited term. Nor may he buy or sell in any market, fair, or place of public sale. The same principle applies to the cultivation of so large an amount of glebe as to divert all the parson's energies to secular matters. It is not well that he should be looking after a sick calf when he ought to be looking after a sick parishioner. But now that British agriculture has fallen so low that tenants are unprocurable, the incumbent, unless prepared to resign, or to let the glebe go out of cultivation, has often no option but to farm it himself, and an enormous amount of private capital has in the aggregate been expended by incumbents on the purchase of live and dead stock for farms unexpectedly thrown on their hands, although they must be conscious that cultivation which has failed to pay when directed by an expert is still less likely to answer in the hands of an amateur.

The ordinary result is such as may be inferred from the following statements made in 1884 to a Committee of Convocation by incumbents farming their own glebe. "Little or no profit." "Average yearly loss of £100." "Farmed at a loss of rent, rates, and taxes." "Income at present less than none." "Land has cost for cleaning, etc., £100 per annum out of private income." "Unless assistance offered, soon be ruined." "Expect to have to retire from loss year by year." "Lost £1500 out of £2000; glebe now let." It is significant that in the comparatively small area, including only eight archdeaconries, to which the investigations of the Committee extended, there were, even in 1884, no less than sixty cases in which incumbents had been forced to find capital for farming their glebe lands, with the only alternative of letting them go to utter waste. This number has presumably been largely increased during the last three years; and most of the capital thus expended has unquestionably been utterly lost. No doubt a glebe owner is severely handicapped in this matter, especially from the fact that, although his is a limited tenure, he is not entitled by law to any compensation for unexhausted improvements. But with this and other legal hardships by which he is affected, I shall deal separately.

CHAPTER III.

THE DIOCESE OF LINCOLN.

IT is a great pity that more care is not taken, when statistics are being collected for Parliament, to ensure their being given on some uniform plan. "It would be well to arrange your facts in some order, even alphabetical order, if you cannot think of any other," was Mr. Justice Maule's sneer when a member of the junior bar was floundering before him; and haphazard statistics are worse even than higgledy-piggledy arguments. A Blue-book which has lately been issued by the Home Office is a striking example of confusion. It professes to give a return of all glebe lands in England and Wales, with their annual value, and the parishes in which they are situate. Unfortunately, it is obvious from internal evidence that the instructions issued with the return were not successful in securing that the "annual value" should be based on that settled by the local Assessment Committee. The column in which it is stated is headed "gross estimated rental," and it is clear that in many cases the figures given are merely conventional, and represent not what the rental now is, but what it was in prosperous times.[1] If, instead of the "gross estimated rental," each incumbent had been required to state the average rent actually received in the last three years, or, where the glebe is in hand, the amount of the poor-law assessment; if agricultural land had been distinguished from house property; and if the value of parsonage and garden, instead of being sometimes inserted and sometimes omitted, had been stated separately, the return would have been a very valuable contribution to the land questions which are coming more and more to the fore. But the compilers of the form of return, with unconscious humour, provided another trap for the unwary parson, by requiring him to state the "poor-law parish wherein glebe is situate." Now, everybody understands the meaning of a "civil parish" and of an "ecclesiastical parish," but people may be excused for not knowing what is a "poor-law parish." Parishes existed before poor-laws, and the poor-laws did not create parishes, but unions. The result of the use of this term was that a considerable proportion of the incumbents did not mention the parish in which the glebe is situate, but merely

---

[1] In one case, the "annual value" of glebe, which for some years has been rented at £600, is given as £900 (the old rent); in another instance, where the rent last year was under £200, and most of the land is going out of cultivation, the "annual value" is stated as £440.

the poor-law union, and thus in many instances the return gives nothing more than that vague indication of locality. Defective as it is, however, it supplies some useful information, and an abstract (see Appendix B), in which are given the number of livings in each diocese, and the average amount of land attached to each living, will convey some notion of the differences which exist as regards the amount of glebe in various parts of the country.

Among other things the return shows, on comparison with the Clergy List, that in the diocese of Lincoln, with which I propose specially to deal in the present chapter, something like one-third of the incumbents derive practically their whole income from glebe, and that at least another third depend upon that resource for a considerable part of their emoluments. The average amount of glebe held by each of the 586 incumbents is no less than 116 acres, the annual value of which is stated in the return as £1 5s. 8d. per acre, though I have good reason to believe that this estimate is excessive. In several cases the farms attached to the benefices are 600 or 700 acres in extent, and a large number are between 200 and 300 acres.

The ordinary depreciation in agricultural rentals in Lincolnshire during the last few years, as I learn from trustworthy sources, ranges between 30 and 50 per cent., and this applies alike to clerical and lay landowners. But here, as in Nottinghamshire, tenants are becoming scarce, and both squires and parsons are in many instances unable to let their land. I was told, though I cannot vouch for the fact, that Lord Aveland, who is one of the largest landowners in the county, has over 10,000 acres in hand, and I heard of many clergymen who were farming their own glebes with small success, and of a few cases in which the land had actually been allowed to go out of cultivation.

In one living, formerly worth £800 a year, which was mainly derived from a glebe of nearly 500 acres, the farm is now abandoned, the fields are merely roughly ploughed and left to produce a jungle forming an excellent cover for partridges, but not paying for the growth of corn. The land is a stiff clay, and used to produce heavy crops, but only with an expenditure for labour which would not be repaid by the present price of corn. Several livings are vacant because no one can afford to accept them. As a vicar told me, "It has come to this, that no one without good private means can afford to take a country living dependent on glebe, unless he wishes speedily to pass through the bankruptcy court." One benefice, which is in the gift of the Lord Chancellor, has 240 acres of glebe and a house, and used to be worth £350 a year. Large sums were spent for farm buildings and drainage, but nevertheless the land, instead of fetching 30s. an acre, now only fetches 6s. 6d., and the result is that the interest on one mortgage to Queen Anne's Bounty, and on another to a land improvement company, considerably exceeds the revenue, and it has not yet been possible to find a clergyman ready to pay something like £100 a year for the honour of being rector. In another case, the value of a vicarage which used to be worth about £200 a year has been reduced, by the fall in the value of land, and by charges for damages mainly caused by floods, to something like £50, and, as there is no parsonage, it has been vacant for several years. In a third instance, the nominal value of a vicarage is £180, but as the receipt of that sum depends upon a glebe of about 70 acres which cannot be let, this parish, too, is without an incumbent, and seems likely to remain so. In several cases, what were rich benefices have had part of their income diverted to poor ones, and the result is that as the rents of their glebes have gone down they have now little left for themselves. The living of T., for example, has nearly 700 acres of glebe, which used to produce over £1000 a year, and it was thought desirable, eight or ten years ago, to appropriate £350 of this income to a neighbouring living. There are charges for repayment of loans for house and farm buildings which amount to £211 annually, so the total deductions from income, irrespective of rates and taxes, are £561; and as the rental of the glebe has fallen to £685, the balance left is only £124, out of which a large rectory with extensive gardens has to be maintained. The same sort of thing has happened in some other cases, and so the attempt to equalize the value of different livings has not been successful. There are, indeed, substantial objections to the practice. In the first place, it is not desirable, without overwhelming necessity, to appropriate to one benefice the revenue designed for and raised in another; and, in the second place, it is not expedient that all benefices should be reduced to the same dead level. As the Bishop of Nottingham remarked to me on this subject, "We have uneven men, and we want uneven livings."

On the whole, however, notwithstanding the existence of individual cases of severe hardship, I am inclined to think that the clergy of Lincolnshire are better off than their brethren in some other parts of the Midlands. This is due in a large degree to the operations of the Diocesan Society for the Augmentation of Poor Livings, which was established by Bishops Wordsworth and Trollope, and which in the course of the last sixteen years has locally raised no less a sum than £77,000. It has been the aim of the society to get its grants supplemented both by the patrons of the livings and by the Governors of Queen Anne's Bounty, and the system has worked in this way. If the owner of the advowson of a living wishes to augment it, and is willing to contribute, say £200, for the purpose, the society meets that grant with another £200. Then the £400 thus provided is placed in the hands of the Governors of Queen Anne's Bounty, who, according to their usual rule, add to it a corresponding sum, and thereafter the incumbent receives the interest of £800, not dependent on tithes or glebe, but regularly paid to him in cash by the Bounty Office.

It is no doubt a wonderful thing to have been able to raise something like £5000 a year in a single diocese for this purpose, and the result is due in a great measure to the energy and influence of Bishop Trollope, whose own liberality is unbounded, and whose recent gift of £5000 for the restoration of the Minster Hall at Southwell only represents a small proportion of his contributions to Church objects. He has, however, been well supported by the clergy, a large proportion of whom have private resources. In Lincolnshire, perhaps more than elsewhere, it used to be a matter of course for one of the younger sons of each of the county families to take Orders, and the Church thus gained both in means and in influence. It has been estimated that throughout the county no less than half the different funds raised for all charitable purposes is contributed by the clergy. Fortunately, in many districts the glebe is largely composed of excellent pasture, which has not depreciated in value in anything like the same degree as the arable land.

There has been no exceptional difficulty in collecting tithe, and no agitation of consequence against its payment. Of course, the arrears have been greater than in prosperous times, but the existence of livings dependent upon glebe by the side of livings dependent upon tithes is an excellent corrective of the notion that tenants would gain by the abolition of tithe rent-charge. In one parish, where land is subject to a tithe of 5*s.* an acre, it fetches a rent of 20*s.* In the adjoining parish, where the land is tithe free, it fetches 25*s.* It is quite clear, then, that the difference due to the absence of tithe goes into the pocket, not of the tenant, but of the landlord, and this was in effect the view taken by the Lincolnshire Chamber of Agriculture when it recently discussed the subject.

In the diocese of Lincoln, as I had found to be the case in Southwell, the clergy who have tried to farm their own glebe have generally made a sad mess of it for want of knowledge and often of capital. If there is one thing more certain than another, it is that in these days farming must be conducted by experts, that it will not bear extra burdens, and that if money has to be borrowed for stock or improvements the result will be inevitable grief. But here, as elsewhere, incumbents have made the attempt in a large number of cases, and have wasted a good deal of their own capital. I am afraid it must be admitted that they have in some instances had farms thrown on their hands because, from the nature of the case, they are by no means good landlords. Theirs is a life interest of a special kind, and yet they have not the legal privileges of ordinary life-owners. They have every temptation to rack-rent their glebe, and every motive to dissuade them from spending money upon it. The tithe-owner generally derives his income from many tithe-payers; the glebe owner, on the other hand, usually has "all his eggs in one basket," and is prompted to act in accordance with what seem to be the exigencies of the moment, rather than on considerations of what is best for the permanent advantage of the living.

Nor has he always had sufficient regard to the future in the expenditure for which he has charged his benefice. It has frequently happened that an incumbent with large private means, or who wishes to take pupils, or who is blessed or afflicted with an exceptionally large family, has built a parsonage out of all proportion to the value of the living, and for that purpose has raised a large amount by mortgage from Queen Anne's Bounty, the result being not only that his successor, if a poor man, finds the payment of the instalments of principal and interest a terrible burden, but that a big house, which has to be kept up and repaired, is an encumbrance which he would gladly exchange for a residence of more modest dimensions. Of course, most of these parsonages are now paid for, just as most of the churches have by this time been restored, and in this respect the incumbents of the present day are luckier than their predecessors. But, on the other hand, the rates and taxes are very high, and are steadily increasing. The extent of many of the parishes is large, and a horse is in such cases an absolute necessity. Perhaps more than one church has to be served, and then a curate must be kept, whose stipend of £130 or £140 a year may make him better off than his rector.

Moreover, people living in large towns have really scarcely any idea of the degree in which the poor in rural parishes depend upon the clergy to supply their various wants. I know of one suburban district in which the labouring classes are so few and the charitable ladies so numerous, that cases of distress are at a great premium, and if an old woman does but sneeze, half a dozen benevolent spinsters are sure to rush at her with pocket-handkerchiefs, jelly, and cough mixture. But in a parish in the Fen country, where there is probably not even a doctor within many miles, everything falls on the parson. The poor apply to him whenever they are in any kind of distress;

it is from the rectory that they look to receive, as a matter of course, not only sick-room comforts, but contributions for Widow Smith, whose furniture has been burnt, for Gaffer Jones, whose only cow has died, and for old Hodge, towards the supply of a successor to that three-legged horse which has finally collapsed, after being for years the means of keeping him and his wife out of the workhouse by the performance of odd jobs of every description.

To many clergymen it is the keenest blow to find themselves absolutely unable any longer, from sheer want of means, to give this sort of help to their parishioners; and the worst of it is that the people are quite incapable of comprehending that it has been possible for poverty to overwhelm their parson, whom they regard as a sort of charitable institution, permanently embodied; who has, according to the unassailable belief of the oldest inhabitants, a fine income; and who was as liberal as former rectors till what they consider to be this fit of stinginess came upon him. They cannot conceive that he now receives from his benefice less than an artisan's wages; and that, perhaps—I have heard of many such cases—he and his family are merely living on the pittance received from relatives and friends. He has bad debts, too, arrears of tithe and of rent of glebe, and if he adopts any legal measures for their recovery, however pressing may be his own necessities, he is held up to opprobrium as "a pretty sort of Christian to take the law of a poor man." Altogether his lot is not a happy one, and, indeed, the temporal advantages of the Church as a profession are so much less than they used to be, that it is no wonder if some falling off is noticeable in the quality of the clerical recruits of late years.

CHAPTER IV.

THE DIOCESE OF ELY.

I HAVE lately been in communication with farmers, glebe-owners, land agents, and other persons interested in agriculture in various parts of England, and it is sad to note the unanimity with which they declare that there are at present no signs of improvement in the business of farming, and the hopelessness with which most of them regard the future. It is useless to represent to them that the prices of wheat, barley, and oats, on which the tithe averages are calculated, were actually lower in 1850 than in 1886; that a series of years in which farmers were prosperous and land was eagerly competed for only ended in 1878; and that what has happened before may reasonably be expected to happen again. It is vain to urge that as England is becoming more and more one large town, with a population rapidly increasing upon an area which cannot increase, it is preposterous to suppose that the land will become valueless prairie rather than, as one would think more likely, either valuable garden or pasture. The rejoinder is an appeal to the undeniable fact that, whatever possibilities may be hidden in the womb of the future, land has for the last ten years been steadily depreciating in value ; tenants are becoming more and more difficult to obtain ; even skilled farmers are losing money, and fields which used to be heavy with golden grain are now left untilled, " a wild where weeds and flowers promiscuous shoot." I have heard, it is true, of a few long-headed persons who are buying up land at its present low price, in confidence that it will recover its old value within a few years, and it is possible that they will make money if they can hold on long enough. I was even told of a case in the Midlands in which one of these investors had bought a farm of 200 acres nine months ago at £20 an acre, and had just let it at 30*s.*, thus obtaining the handsome interest of $7\frac{1}{2}$ per cent. on the capital expended. This was an instance of prompt success, due to judicious selection, and was no doubt exceptional. Still, extraordinary bargains in land are to be picked up every day at the present time, and, despite the croakers, I believe that, for the reasons I have mentioned, people who can afford to wait may find the most profitable investment in a security which cannot run away or be stolen, and which a general European war—no unlikely contingency—would only render more valuable, while it would depress stocks and shares of every kind. Meanwhile, things certainly seem deplorably bad in most parts of England, and especially in the heavy clays of Cambridgeshire and Huntingdon. Here, as already stated, the main resource of the incumbents is glebe, not tithes; and I have been made aware, not of one or two, but of scores of cases in which they are attempting to farm their own land from the sheer impossibility of getting tenants at any price. The result, in nine instances out of ten, is that they are losing whatever capital they possess, and that if they had no private means they would soon be in the bankruptcy court.

In the diocese of Ely, the average amount of glebe is 88 acres to each benefice, and some livings have from 500 to nearly 1000 acres apiece. In the parish of A, the rent ten years ago was £1406; the charges, including rates and taxes, £686 (of which about £400 is for fen drainage); and the curate's stipend £150; leaving a net income of £570. At the present time, the rent, when it is all paid (which seldom happens), is £880, while the outgoings are as before, and the net income, therefore, amounts to the magnificent sum of £44. In parish B, the glebe consists of 508 acres, of which 33 are in grass, and the rest arable, the rent having been formerly £813. For nearly four years, 205 acres were unoccupied; while now, although most of the land is let, the rent has dropped to £390; and as, not long ago, there was a sum of £524 tithe rent-charge in arrear, it may be imagined that this once rich living is not in a flourishing condition. In benefice C, the glebe consists of 270 acres, mostly arable, and fifteen years ago the rent was £500. But since the depression only 100 acres have been let, at £1 per acre, and the incumbent is struggling to maintain a large family on that sum, and on the produce of the remaining 170 acres which he is unable to let, and must farm as well as he can, or, in other words, at a loss. In parish D, the glebe of 436 acres used to fetch £600 a year. Of this, 200 acres are now in hand from the impossibility of getting a tenant, and are bringing in less than the outgoings; 110 acres of grass are let for £110, 28 acres of clover for £10 10s., and a few small pieces for sums which, after payment of all charges, scarcely leave even starvation wages for the rector. In parish E, 355 acres, formerly let at £500, are being farmed by the incumbent at a heavy loss. In parish F, 560 acres which formerly produced £600 are now let at £250, out of which a charge of about £100 a year has to be paid to Queen Anne's Bounty. In parish G, the rent of 245 acres has dropped from £394 to £50, though the rector has sunk £3000 of his own capital on the land, an expenditure of which he will never be recouped one farthing. In parish H, with a glebe of 138 acres, the rent used to be £250, but from 1879 to

1884 only about £50 a year was paid, of which £30 was in kind—butter, eggs, poultry, etc. In 1884, the tenant became bankrupt, owing the rector £800, of which only a very small proportion was received as dividend. Then the rector took the farm into his own hands, placed it in a thoroughly good condition, did much in the way of drainage and repairs, and lost on an average £40 a year, even with no rent to pay. At present he is vainly seeking a tenant at a good deal less than half of the former rent. In parish I, where the income is solely derived from glebe, the incumbent, at the age of eighty-three, found his means of living suddenly reduced from £180 to £40 a year. Another, in very similar circumstances, died heart-broken, not so much from regret at the loss of personal comfort as from distress at being no longer able to help his people; and I could not avoid thinking that, in the words of Eöthen, "the old man had got rather well out of the scrape of being alive and poor."

If it were not for the fear of being wearisome, I could easily give scores of instances within the one diocese of Ely in which the same sort of thing has taken place. I have the names of twenty livings, mostly in Bedfordshire, Suffolk, and Huntingdon, with aggregate glebe of just under 7000 acres, or an average of 350 acres each. Ten years ago, the rental was over £12,000, or about 35s. an acre, the average being £600 apiece. It is now £3731, being less than 11s. an acre, or £186 to each benefice; and even this amount is subject to large deductions for charges of various kinds. If the reader of these lines will picture to himself his own position if his entire income, whatever it may be, were suddenly reduced to one-third of its amount, he will have some notion of the unfortunate position of many of the clergy in what used to be the finest wheat-growing districts in England. But, as the Archdeacon of Huntingdon has said, bare statistics cannot represent the amount of anxiety and privation which have been patiently borne by many a clergyman's family during recent years. In addition to the difficulties consequent on loss of income, the incumbent has often been forced to encounter those of engaging in an occupation for which he has received no previous training, and in which he knows that even experts are losing money on all sides. As the Archdeacon observes, clergymen at the best of times are not particularly good men of business, and one who is forced to embark, perhaps on borrowed capital, on all the intricacies of farming operations, is pretty sure to come to grief. Yet, in default of tenants, it is his only means of subsistence where the benefice consists solely of glebe, as is so often the case in the Midlands. Sometimes, where the land is let, and the tenant finds himself in difficulties, the parson has preferred to suffer in silence rather than add to his parishioner's embarrassment by pressing for the rent.

The sum spent, and lost, by incumbents out of their private resources in the improvement of the land attached to their benefices must be in the aggregate enormous. I have a list of seventeen parishes in the diocese of Ely, in which the clergymen have thus expended altogether no less than £21,173; and it must be remembered that this sum represents an absolute gift to the livings in question, and that, unlike lay agriculturists, neither the incumbents nor their representatives are able to claim either tenant-right or compensation for unexhausted improvements in respect of it. In some cases, money has been laid out in converting arable land into pasture, and the result has now and then been to secure tenants for what was before absolutely unletable. But the expense is very heavy, amounting, according to one estimate which I received, to an average of at least £5 an acre if the work is done thoroughly, to say nothing of the fact that for two or three years the new pasture has to be treated very tenderly, and its full value is therefore not at once obtained. Of course the result is to lessen by about one-half the employment of labour; and a change of this kind, if carried out on a large scale throughout the country, will hasten that depopulation of the rural districts and overcrowding of the towns which has been for some time in progress. Moreover, is it not likely that the diminution in the demand for hands will be followed by a reduction in the rate of wages? At present the remuneration of the labourer in several districts which I have visited is very little below the maximum which it has reached even in times of agricultural prosperity. Over and over again I was told that he has never been better off than at the present time. He can get more for his money than he has ever been able to obtain in the past; he is better housed and better clad than his forefathers; and it may be said of him, as in Virgil's time, that, if he only knew it, his lot is a very fortunate one.

I happened to be in the Ramsey Division of Huntingdon at the time of the recent election, and it was amusing to find the difficulty which the Radical electioneers experienced in making the labourer believe that he was a down-trodden serf, who ought to be discontented, and whose only hope of freedom was to be found in voting for the Radicals, as proposing to give him not only a share of his master's land, but the means of farming it. Was it not owing to Liberal legislation, he was asked, that both corn and clothing were cheap, and was not the great object of the Tories to make them dear again? Why should the squire be dressed in broadcloth, and the man who made the squire's fortune be compelled to wear corduroy? Fortunately, however, Hodge was too sagacious to believe nonsense of this kind, and he even, to use Mr. Stephen's phrase, placed the tongue of incredulity in the cheek of derision when such political pabulum was offered for his consumption. The vapourings of the Irish orators who infested the Huntingdonshire villages were not left to work their effect without some statements of fact on the other side. Some hardy spirits ventured even to argue that the present cheapness of the necessaries of life has resulted, not so much from the absence of taxation on imported articles as on the increase in the means of distribution by railways and steamships, this presumption being strengthened by the cases of France and Germany, where, though both are Protectionist countries, prices are at least as low as in England. As to the Disestablishment of the Church, the labourers refused altogether the bait held out to them. Many of them had suffered from the ruin of the farmers and the squires; and if the clerical resident in each parish, uniting in himself some of the functions of each class, were to be driven away, they failed to see how they would benefit, or what good it would do them to cut off the usual help from the rectory. So, on the whole, they decided to return the Conservative candidate.

CHAPTER V.

THE DIOCESE OF PETERBOROUGH.

THE diocese of Peterborough was the first to feel acutely the effect of the agricultural depression. It comprises the counties of Northampton, Leicester, and Rutland, and, therefore, includes a very large amount of heavy land, which used to fetch a high rent before wheat was brought as ballast from America, but which often costs too much for cultivation to leave even the smallest margin for the landlord at present prices. Here, as I have mentioned previously, the incomes of the clergy are mainly derived from the glebes which were assigned to them in lieu of tithes under the old Enclosure Acts, and many of which are very large. Ten livings have over 500 acres of land each, and the aggregate amount is no less than 74,632 acres, which is more than one-ninth of the whole amount of glebe in England and Wales, and is not even approached by any other diocese except Lincoln. The contrast between this and a tithe-paying diocese may be judged from the fact to which I have already referred, that in Peterborough the average area of glebe attached to each living is 129 acres, while in Rochester it is little more than five acres.

As long ago as 1881, the fall in the rent of the land was so generally felt that a committee was appointed by the Diocesan Conference to report on the matter, and this committee collected returns from 336 incumbents. Even then it was found that 9373 acres were on the hands of 79 clergy from inability to find tenants, and that glebe rents had undergone a reduction of about 25 per cent. between 1870 and 1880. There were two disadvantages which had been felt in a good many cases—first, that there was too much arable land in proportion to grass, a good deal of old pasture having been improvidently ploughed up when wheat was dear; and, secondly, that there was often no dwelling-house (apart from the parsonage), and sometimes not even any farm buildings, on the glebe, so that it could not be let separately, and was therefore at the mercy of the neighbouring farmer. Then, the committee found reason to believe that although very large sums had been expended on the land, either from the private resources of the incumbents, or by means of loans from Queen Anne's Bounty and land improvement companies, yet, partly through the operation of the Dilapidations Acts, and partly from the clergy's inexperience, a large proportion of the money had been wasted.

The report of this committee is interesting, as showing both the special remedies suggested by those who had been hit hardest by the depression, and the view taken of these suggestions by the committee, which numbered among its members not only clergymen, but such practical men of business as Mr. Albert Pell and Mr. Heygate. First, of course, came complaints of the burdens imposed by the repayment of loans granted by the governors of Queen Anne's Bounty for land improvements; but the committee recognized the fact that, although particular cases might deserve special leniency, a wholesale reduction of the rate of interest would not be desirable, as it would be by no means an advantage to the Church to cripple the hands of the governors in their ordinary work of augmenting poor benefices. It was considered, however, that the instalments of principal might reasonably be spread over a larger number of years, and, as I have already stated, the governors have obtained special legislative power, in the session just past, to afford this measure of relief. A good many of the clergy were anxious to have the power of handing over their glebe to be managed by the Ecclesiastical Commissioners, on condition of receiving from them a stipend calculated, on the same principle as tithe, upon the average net rental of the preceding seven years. It was urged that this scheme would be advantageous by substituting for the inexperienced management of the parsons the skilled management of the commissioners' agents; that it would give the tenant a better security for his holding, which now is usually dependent on the life of the incumbent, and would thus lead to better farming; and, finally, that a similar arrangement had been found to answer in the case of episcopal estates. The committee, however, refused to recommend any such general transfer of Church lands, mainly on account of the difficulty, expense, and danger of centralization, the loss of the benefit arising from resident landowners, the growing jealousy against the accumulation of land in the hands of large corporations, and the possible suggestiveness of such a course to a policy of confiscation. The question of a sale of glebe was much discussed, but the committee were adverse to this step, except in extreme cases. In the first place, it must be remembered that if all glebe had been sold at the prices of a couple of hundred years ago, and the proceeds had been then invested, the income, according to the present value of money, would be insignificant; and it is unreasonable to suppose that land will never recover from the existing depression, or that a pound fifty years hence will be worth as much as a pound at the present time. Then, in ordinary circumstances, the greatest pressure to sell glebe would be in cases where no tenants could be found, and where the land would, therefore, fetch very little. Finally, some of the committee insisted on the advantage of there being an independent landowner in every parish, and of maintaining this secular side of the clergy's position. But still the fact was recognized that to make a living out of land was getting progressively more difficult.

Since 1882, when this report appeared, things have been getting worse and worse in a large part of the diocese of Peterborough. As for the grazing districts of Leicester and Rutland, they have suffered heavily enough, the rents of pasture having fallen at least 15 or 20 per cent. in the last ten years. But the value of the arable land of Northamptonshire has depreciated in a much larger degree—how much it is impossible to estimate with accuracy, since in many instances tenants cannot be obtained at any price. I have, however, particulars of twenty benefices in that county, with an aggregate amount of 3789 acres of glebe which are still let, or, at any rate, were not without tenants a short time ago. The glebe used to fetch £7772, being an average of over £2 an acre, or £388 to each benefice. It now produces £3553, being less than 19s. an acre, or £177 to each benefice This statement, indeed, rather under-estimates the present extent of loss in those particular instances, for it is mainly founded on returns collected by Archdeacon Lightfoot for a committee of Convocation more than a couple of years ago, and rents have become still lower in the interval.

Nor has the case of clergymen forced to farm their own glebe undergone any improvement. It would be easy to add scores of instances, such as I have given with regard to the diocese of Ely, in which incumbents have been reduced to the greatest straits from having been forced into the very complicated business of farming. Two or three typical cases will, however, be sufficient. In one parish, there is no income for the rector except such as may be derived from a glebe of 440 acres, which used to bring in a rental of £695 per annum. Of this, 245 acres are now let at £240, a sum which is nearly swallowed up by charges for repayment of loans to Queen Anne's Bounty Office, and a land improvement company. The remaining 195 acres are in hand, and the rector has laid out £1000 of his private capital on farming them. But he is unable to do so with success; and the so-called "living" is, therefore, worth rather less than nothing. In a second parish, glebe which used to fetch a rental of £195 is in hand, but, far from producing a profit, has lately been costing the unfortunate rector £100 a year out of his private income. In a third parish, where the rent of the glebe used to be £500, the incumbent is also trying to farm it, as he can get no tenant, and he has expended £4000 of his private capital with the result that he expects soon to be ruined. In another case, the income has sunk from £295 to £111, much of the land having been for some years unlet and uncultivated.

And it must be remembered that this involuntary conversion of parsons into farmers has inevitably involved a very large expenditure of money from their private resources. The business of agriculture is one into which it is impossible to enter without capital. Some large landed proprietors refuse to let a farm to any applicant who is not possessed of at least £8 an acre; and it may be said, generally, that to enter on a farm of 200 acres not much less than £2000 is required. More than two years ago, it was estimated that, in the diocese of Peterborough alone, incumbents, who were compelled to farm their own glebe, had spent from their private means no less than £50,000; and it is to be feared that not only has most of this capital been lost, but the same process of expending and losing is still going on, and "good money is being thrown after bad." Where tenants are obtained it is too often the case that they have not sufficient means, and, after starving the land for a year or two, they leave without paying their rent. In fact, as it was tersely put to me by an experienced land agent, men of substance are being replaced by men of straw.

On the other hand, I am bound to say that one of my informants, who from his position had the means of forming a good opinion on the subject, was inclined to think that though the new tenants had less money than the old, and rented much smaller holdings, they were more hard-working, and bore more resemblance to the old English yeomen, who were not ashamed to be seen at the plough's tail, and whose wives and daughters looked after the dairy. "Do not think," he said, "that I join in the senseless abuse of farmers for following the hounds instead of the harrow, and for letting their daughters learn to play the piano instead of churning butter. The tenant-farmer is often worth £5000 or £10,000, and has a perfect right to enjoy sport, and to have his children educated as well as those of any other man of similar means. But I believe in spade husbandry as well as in steam ploughs, and it is by no means a bad thing to have a number of small farms cultivated by men who will force the land to pay, and will spend their utmost energies in the effort, for the simple reason that it is their only means of subsistence. Land hunger exists in England as well as in Ireland, and it is just as well to satisfy it when possible." Farms under 50 acres can now be let much more easily than those of greater extent, partly, no doubt, because those who have lost money in large holdings are obliged to begin again on a smaller scale, and partly also because men of the labouring class who have somehow acquired a little money are anxious to go into business on their own account.

As to allotments, I am certain, from the results of my inquiries in various parts of England, that the demand for them has been much exaggerated. In fact, almost everywhere land is such a drug in the market that tenants of any kind have been at a premium. If owners, whether lay or clerical, can let their land as allotments, they are not silly enough to refuse. As to the likelihood that sanitary authorities will take land compulsorily for the purpose, *credat Judæus.* When there was an outcry as to the housing of the poor, one of the chief measures of relief provided by Sir Charles Dilke's Act consisted in the investment of rural authorities with power to provide labourers' cottages; but I believe that I am correct in saying that this power has not been exercised in a single instance. The same thing will happen as regards the provision of allotments. The authorities will do nothing in the matter: first, because they do not wish to become landlords, and secondly, because the labourer who wants an allotment can easily get one without their interference. As regards the relations of the clergy and the labourers on this matter, I believe that, at any rate in the Midlands, most of the allotments are on glebe; and I have heard of several cases in which the land used for this purpose is the only part of the glebe which is let.

CHAPTER VI.

GLEBES GENERALLY.

It was only about nine years ago that an estate, comprising some of the finest wheat-growing land in England, was professionally valued by one of the best known land agents in London. His report was to the effect that at a forced sale it might not fetch more than £500,000, but that if disposed of judiciously it would command not less than £600,000, and, on the whole, he considered that the value might fairly be taken as £550,000. It was, however, not then offered for sale; and the same land agent has just revalued it. His report is to the effect that a purchaser might possibly be found to give £200,000, but that this is the utmost which it would bring. Nor does this loss of between 60 and 70 per cent. by the landowner adequately represent the difference between 1878 and 1887. The farms were then occupied by prosperous yeomen, and gave occupation to many hundreds of labourers. Now, the farmers are being ruined, and, as the labour bill is the one which most easily admits of indefinite reduction, the men are being discharged, to pick up a precarious living in the already crowded towns, or to swell the ranks of the unemployed. The only chance for the estate seems to be to lay down in grass a large portion of the magnificent arable land which has this year been growing some of the heaviest wheat crops in the country, but which, however abundant the harvest, is not worth cultivating at present prices. It is doubtful, however, whether it would repay the serious cost of conversion into pasture. The price of stock is almost unprecedentedly low ; and the facilities of transport from abroad, both in the case of cattle and of fresh meat, are increasing every year. Altogether the outlook is terribly black, and it is quite conceivable that in a few years much of that land, and thousands of acres like it, may be absolutely out of cultivation. When it is objected that our fiscal policy may have something to do with the prevailing depression, we are generally told that protectionist nations are suffering much more than ourselves. It would be interesting to learn whether either France or Germany could supply an instance in which a considerable tract of exceptionally rich agricultural land has in nine years been reduced to a third of its value, and where the only possibility of maintaining it in cultivation seems to involve its being practically depopulated. Anybody who has noticed the pains bestowed in Switzerland upon the cultivation of every patch of soil that clings to the mountain side; who has seen the extent to which enormous sandy tracts of country in North Germany are carefully tilled by hand labour; and who knows how, alike on the Roumanian border in the South, and on the Polish frontier in the North, agriculture flourishes in Hungary, and employs the labour of an enormous population on the rocky flanks of the Carpathians, may well wonder whether it is necessary that some of the best land in Europe should become a waste because it happens to be situated in England. Of course, wages are low on the Continent, and the labourer is content with a much lower standard of living than in this country. But the instance which I have given is one which may be commended to the notice of political economists.

I fear it is an illustration, on a scale which is by no means insignificant, of what is going on in many parts of England. In my inquiries as to the condition of the glebe-owners in Cambridgeshire, Northamptonshire, and Lincolnshire, I heard over and over again of cases where the value of land has been reduced in at least an equal degree, and I have lately received letters from clergymen in many other counties, all telling the same piteous tale. Here are some cases of what used to be exceptionally rich livings. The incumbent of a parish in the West of England has glebe which used to produce between £800 and £900 a year. At the present time, 220 acres, or more than one-half, are tenantless and uncultivated; the rent has sunk to £426, and, what with rates and taxes (£60), payment to Queen Anne's Bounty (over £100), repairs (£38), and other necessary outgoings, the net income is reduced to £136, out of which, after payment of insurance and doctors' bills, there is not much left for the bare necessaries of life. The incumbent himself performs the whole of either three or four services at different churches in his parish every Sunday, and has been accustomed for many years to treat his choir, school teachers, district visitors, and other Church workers, with a generous hand, while he has largely supported the parochial charities; and I really believe that he feels his present poverty less for his own sake than for theirs. And if we look at the matter from a wider point of view, there seems to be something wrong in a system under which, in a single parish, a couple of hundred acres of arable land, which used to produce much corn and employ much labour, are now a prairie, unproductive and depopulated. In another case a large glebe of about 1000 acres used to let for £1600 a year. Now just half is let for £360, and the other half is, in default of a tenant, being farmed by the rector with the degree of success that usually attends amateur agriculture. In a neighbouring parish, the income from land has dropped from £360 a year to a sum not quite sufficient to pay the pension of £80 on which the previous incumbent retired, yet even there a clergyman with small private means is cheerfully performing the duties of his cure for a remuneration which is rather less than nothing. In a more favourable instance, in which there is a glebe of nearly 1100 acres, the rent used to be £2300. It is now much less than half that amount, and as three curates have to be kept at an aggregate cost of nearly £400 a year, and there are heavy charges for payments to Queen Anne's Bounty, rates, taxes, and various parochial objects, it is only by the expenditure of considerable private means that the work of the Church is maintained in this once rich benefice.

In one living, with between 600 and 700 acres of glebe, the net income has fallen to £300, as compared with £515 ten years ago, and the number of labourers employed has been reduced by one-half; in another, the rent of over 800 acres has gone down from £900 to £600, although these two are in a south-western county, where the depression is much less than in some other parts of England. In another living, with over 1000 acres of glebe, the net income used to be about £700. Three years ago, one farm was thrown on the rector's hands, with the result of a loss of £400; in the following year, it was let again, but at a reduction of 50 per cent., and last year, after payment of a curate and a scripture reader, the rector's net income was £75. In another case, the rent of a large glebe was formerly £872. A few years ago, two holdings were thrown on the rector's hands, and were farmed by him at a loss of £600, to say nothing of £1000, borrowed from a land improvement company, which remains a charge on the benefice. Now the rent has fallen to £476, and is likely to fall much lower, as one tenant has given notice to quit unless land formerly let at £1 an acre is leased to him at 2s. 6d. And the worst of it is that some of the tenants are starving the land; the result being that when a farm is thrown up, a large expenditure of capital is necessary in order to bring it again into a proper state of cultivation. In this case, too, scarcely any labour is employed by the tenants, except that of their own families, and perhaps an extra hand or two for haymaking and harvest. In this, as in many other cases already mentioned, I have been supplied with detailed accounts of receipts and outgoings, and my thanks are due to a large number of incumbents for the freedom with which they have afforded me information on the subject, with the sole reservation that, for obvious reasons, their names should not be made public.

I might easily have multiplied the instances which I have given in illustration of the enormous fall in the value of livings, but I have thought it quite enough to take a few cases as typical of the kind of hardship which, in a greater or less degree, has befallen hundreds—if not thousands—of incumbents. I have hitherto confined myself mainly to the subject of glebe, and it may be convenient, before proceeding to that of tithe, to refer to some of the difficulties specially experienced by clerical landholders, and to the legislation which has been proposed for dealing with them. The question is a very large one. The glebe lands in England and Wales amount altogether to 660,000 acres, and in particular districts in the Midlands they constitute something like one-twelfth of the whole area under cultivation. The clergy, it should be remembered, are between one-third and one-fourth of the whole number of resident landowners throughout the country. But their position as regards the cultivation of their lands is far more unfavourable than that of their lay brethren.

Here is an instance of what frequently happens. A glebe is thrown up by a tenant who has impoverished the land, and the incumbent has no alternative but to farm it himself. He spends his own capital upon it, and having by this means brought it into a good state of cultivation, so as again to command a fair rent, he is obliged, either from ill health or on promotion, to resign his benefice. Under the present law, not only has he no claim for compensation for "unexhausted improvements," but he is not even entitled to the value of the growing crops which he has himself sown. As was pointed out by a committeee of Convocation in 1885, an incumbent, no matter how much he may have improved his land, has no remedy against his successor, and on quitting his land can claim no such reimbursement as law and custom give to an ordinary tenant. If the land is let, he has to pay compensation when the tenant quits it; but when he is practically himself the tenant of the benefice he is liable to the loss of everything that he spends upon it. A bill was introduced last session to remedy this manifest injustice, by providing that on the death or resignation of an incumbent he or his representatives might claim from his successor compensation for unexhausted improvements of the kind specified in the Agricultural Holdings Act, and might require growing crops to be taken at a valuation; and also by giving the representatives of a deceased incumbent power to continue to farm the glebe for six months after his death at a rent equivalent to the poor-law assessment, so as to place them, in respect of growing crops, in the same position as tenants holding under limited owners of settled lands. This bill, however, though designed to remedy an obvious injustice, and interfering with nobody's rights, was mischievously blocked, and never got beyond a second reading in the House of Commons. It will, I believe, be again introduced next session, and there ought to be no difficulty in carrying it into law.

As regards Lord Cross's bill with regard to the sale of glebe lands, which also had to be dropped last session, I have heard doubts expressed in several quarters as to whether it would not have done more harm than good. The result might have been that the best land would be sold, and that the incumbent would be left with the worst, which could not be let at all without the other. Any forced sales at the present time would be disastrous. It is true that, as was well put in the report of Archdeacon Lightfoot's Committee of Convocation, the burdens imposed on incumbents by the Ecclesiastical Dilapidations Act, the Agricultural Holdings Act, and the increased charges on land, together with constant anxiety about tenants, the bargaining with parishioners as to rent, the uncertainty of payment, and the possibility of having to farm impoverished lands without any tenant-right, combine to render glebe a far more unsatisfactory source of income than other kinds of property; and where purchasers on advantageous terms can be found, it is well that the land should be sold and the proceeds invested. But this can be done under the existing law, and I recently heard of a case in Lincolnshire in which two neighbouring squires had competed for the purchase of some glebe land, with the ultimate result of providing a largely increased income for the benefice. I doubt whether it is necessary to afford further facilities for the purpose, or whether it is reasonable that the patron's consent should be dispensed with. Individual cases of hardship, arising from the fall of income to an amount insufficient to provide a bare maintenance for the incumbent, might be met by grants from the Ecclesiastical Commissioners; and I see no reason why such grants should not be made on a sliding scale, with provision for their diminution if the rents again rise. The rules at present seem rather too rigid; and the plan suggested would enable relief to be given to the incumbent of a living while the glebe is unletable, without the danger of permanently devoting Church funds to a benefice which may hereafter again become too ample to need augmentation.

CHAPTER VII.

TITHES.

I THINK it is in one of Shirley Brooks's sparkling novels that the heroine is described as one of those people who cannot hear the organ in church without feeling that they would like to be very good. It is not impossible that impulses of this kind may largely account for one fortunate circumstance in the condition of the clergy, namely, that so very many of them who have badly endowed livings have well-endowed wives. I presume that it often happens that a lady possessed of a decent competence is brought by a sermon to the conviction that she ought to employ her worldly means for the good of her fellow-creatures, and the simplest and most obvious way of carrying out this good resolution seems to be to marry the preacher. The result is that in hundreds, or even thousands, of English parishes the clergyman and his family spend much more than they receive from the Church. And in the present position of affairs it is extremely fortunate that the incumbent should ordinarily not be solely dependent upon the revenue of his cure. I fancy that the prevalent notion of the average value of a living is enormously exaggerated, and that few people are aware of the fact that of the 13,800 benefices in England and Wales, between one-third and one-half are even nominally worth less than £200 a year. I have shown the enormous extent to which these nominal incomes have been reduced in the case of livings dependent mainly on glebe, and in the dioceses of Peterborough and Ely alone I have given particulars of forty livings which ten years ago averaged between £600 and £700 in annual value, but which now average less than £180. In many of these cases this reduction has involved something very like ruin to the incumbent ; for it must be remembered that his necessary outgoings do not decrease with his income, and that there is probably no class of men whose net receipts bear so small a proportion to their gross income as the parochial clergy.

No doubt those incumbents who are mainly dependent on tithe have suffered much less than the glebe-owners. In some instances I am inclined to think that they have even been better off than the average lay landowner. Yet any man who was presented to a tithe-living in 1878, which was then worth £337 a year (this being, as we have seen, a much better living than the average), is now receiving only £262, and the difference may, in many cases, represent just the margin between comfort and comparative poverty. The books of life-insurance offices would tell a sad tale of clergymen who have had to mortgage their insurances, or even to sacrifice the premiums paid, and to give up the hope of making provision for their families from sheer inability to find money for the purpose; many have discharged most, if not all, of their servants, while in some cases, where a scattered parish makes a horse almost indispensable, that means of locomotion has had to be given up. And in two ways, as Dr. Jessopp has pointed out in his " Arcadia," the clergy of the present day are worse off than their predecessors. In the first place, it used to be a common practice for the country clergyman to supplement his income by taking pupils. But nowadays educational competition is too great for any arrangement of this kind. Everybody now runs his son for a scholarship, and sends him to be crammed, not by the rector of Muddleton-in-the-Marsh, but by the London coach who has the greatest reputation for imparting, not old-fashioned scholarship, but the best devices for passing modern examinations. Then, it must be admitted that whereas a large proportion of the honour men of Oxford and Cambridge used to take Orders and join the ranks of the country clergy, those with the best degrees are now usually attracted to secular pursuits, and a good many parsons are by no means qualified to coach their squire's son, who has been in the sixth form at Winchester, and is going in for honours. Of course there are notable exceptions, and, for some boys and young men, quiet study in a country parsonage may be much better than the strain of cram and competition elsewhere. But there are many more parsons who want pupils than pupils who want clerical tutors, as may be judged from the fact, for which I can personally vouch, that a single advertisement for home teaching in a clergyman's family for a backward boy recently attracted no less than 146 applications, although the terms offered were exceedingly moderate. Then, as regards the education of their own children, the parsons of the present day have lost the advantage enjoyed by those of a quarter of a century ago. It used to be a common practice at several schools to admit clergymen's sons on reduced terms. At Marlborough, for instance, I believe that thirty years ago any such boy was educated for between £60 and £70 a year. He has now no advantage in that respect over the son of a layman, and his school bills probably exceed £100 a year, though it must be remembered that Marlborough is a school which was specially founded with a view of providing cheap education for the benefit of the parsons. It is true that a number of scholarships are reserved for sons of clergymen, but this merely means that the children of rich fathers are benefited, since only those who can afford to spend money for a course of coaching from professional crammers have much chance of success.

Serious as is the diminution which has already taken place in the incomes of the clergy, it seems certain to become progressively lower. The value of £100 of tithe rent-charge calculated, according to law, on the corn averages of the last seven years, is now £87 8s. 10d. But if calculated on the prices of last September, it would be about £69 15s.; and there are plenty of croakers, by no means wanting in common sense, who are confident that those prices are not likely to be exceeded in future. If so, a living worth £337 in 1878, and £262 in 1887, will be worth scarcely more than £200 in 1894. If, as has been suggested, steamboats, railroads, and telegraph wires make the whole civilized world one community, it is not unreasonable to suppose that land like that of England may be unable to compete with the cornfields of America, where rent and rates scarcely enter into calculation, or with those of India, where labour costs comparatively nothing. Thousands of acres of what was formerly excellent wheat-growing land are now out of cultivation in this country, and already in some cases tithes have disappeared from this cause. As more and more land is allowed to go into waste, the loss to the Church will increase, and the future outlook is certainly very dark from a money point of view.

It is unnecessary, however, to anticipate. The present state of affairs is bad enough, though hitherto there has been, so far as I can ascertain, comparatively little organized opposition to the payment of tithe on this side of the Welsh border. No doubt there have been isolated instances in which payment has been refused and distraint has been invited for the sake of enlisting hostility to the charge, but agitation of this sort has been for the most part discountenanced by the common sense of the majority, and has generally been regarded as a political diversion on the part of some notoriety hunter. The farmers are, as a rule, sufficiently shrewd to see that the tithe rent-charge is a landlord's tax, and that if it were abolished tomorrow the persons to gain would be the landowners, not the tenants. Still, there are not wanting signs that the movement may spread. "We are waiting for Wales," is an expression which I have heard once or twice from agriculturists. In Essex, an attack on tithe rent-charge was organized so long ago as in 1881, and a hostile resolution was carried in the Essex Chamber of Agriculture, the members of which tried to obtain the support of Mr. Chamberlain when President of the Board of Trade, but were warned by him that the alteration which they desired would profit them nothing. Last year, however, the question was again taken up in the Chamber, and a resolution for the readjustment of the tithe was carried after two adjournments. Great bitterness of feeling was manifested, very violent language was used, and the example of Wales was held up for imitation. It is fair to say, however, that the Chamber is believed by no means to represent fairly the general feeling of Essex farmers in the matter, having passed under the control of some exceedingly active Radical Dissenters, who are allowed to carry matters with a high hand.

As a general rule, even in Essex, where agricultural matters are, perhaps, at their worst, tithe has been paid without much question, though in many instances, especially in the case of lay impropriators, reductions have been asked for and sometimes conceded. There seems to be greater willingness to pay the clergyman if, as they say, "he wants it," but some incumbents known to be well off have a good deal of difficulty in collecting it. In one parish, Guy's Hospital, owning the great tithes, distrained on a particular farmer, who agreed with the others to stand out and see what came of it. In this case there was a somewhat riotous auction, but the sale was effected, and the rest of the tithes were collected. It is noticeable that here the vicar's tithes had been paid without question. Near Andover, there was not long ago a somewhat similar distraint on the part, I believe, of the Winchester Chapter, with a sale at which there were some inflammatory speeches; but the agitation in that neighbourhood does not seem to have spread. In Norfolk, there was an instance of the same sort a few months ago; and at Northwich, in Cheshire, an auction after distraint was this autumn made the occasion for an anti-tithe demonstration. But these are only isolated cases, and tolerably extensive inquiries have satisfied me that the movement has not yet made much head, except in Wales and on the Welsh border, though there is no doubt increasing difficulty in collection, and the arrears are probably more considerable than at any previous time.

The relative rents of tithe-free and titheable land of the same character, existing side by side, furnish, as already remarked, the plainest proof of the fallacy of supposing that it is the tenant who would gain by abolition, since the rent of the former exceeds that of the latter by just the amount of the tithe rent-charge. The case was very well stated by the Ecclesiastical Commissioners in the leaflet which they recently issued to the Welsh farmers. There they pointed out that tithe rent-charge is similar to land tax and income tax, which are only paid by the farmer on behalf of the landlord. The Tithe Act provided that the tenant should deduct the amount from his next payment of rent. But landlords and tenants have in most cases, but not universally, agreed between themselves that instead of the tenant paying a larger rent and deducting from it the tithe rent-charge, he should pay a reduced rent and be responsible for the tithe. By so doing, the tenant has for several years past had the benefit of the fall in the averages, as in fixing the rent it is the "commuted amount" which is deducted, and not the sum payable in any particular year, although the averages may reduce it, as in 1887, by 12 per cent., or, as may happen in the near future, by even 30 per cent.

As to the question of a revaluation of tithe, I presume that the farmers would have utterly refused to consent to any scheme of the kind ten years ago, when they would have certainly lost largely by it; and it is scarcely reasonable that they should advocate it now, when they fancy it would be favourable to them. But would it? If the settlement of 1836 were to be disturbed at all, it would be unreasonable that the averages should be based only on corn, which has decreased in value, and not on other farm products, which have increased. Beef, mutton, butter, cheese, milk, eggs, and potatoes were liable to tithe as well as wheat, barley, and oats, and the useful tables published by the Rev. C. A. Stevens show that the price of such produce has of late years been between 30 and 40 per cent. more than it was in the seven years on which the existing tithe averages were based.[1] It is very improbable, therefore, that the tithe-payer would gain by a revaluation. Indeed, in the opinion of so high an authority as Sir James Caird, if the old principle of participation had continued, the annual income of the Church would have been £2,000,000 greater than it now is. This £2,000,000, as he told the Select Committee on Mr. Inderwick's bill on Extraordinary Tithe, has doubtless gone into the pockets of the landowners. But a general revaluation, whether profitable to the tithe-owner or to the tithe-payer, is scarcely within the sphere of practical politics. The questions of the collection, the incidence, and the redemption of the charge are more pressing, and of them I shall speak in another chapter.

[1] It is often tacitly assumed that these averages are mainly dependent on the price of wheat. This is a mistake. A rise or fall of a shilling per quarter in the price of oats affects the average in about the same degree as a rise or fall of two shillings in that of barley, or of three shillings in that of wheat. The price of oats, then, is what concerns the tithe-owner most nearly; and, luckily, there is reason to believe that it is more likely to rise than that of wheat.

CHAPTER VIII.

TITHES (*continued*).

IN some of the Western States of America there is a phrase which describes a particular class of conscience as a "one duck" conscience. It originated in a now ancient story of a sportsman who boasted that he had killed ninety-nine ducks at a single shot. "Why not say a hundred at once?" asked his hearer. "Sir," was the indignant reply, "I reckon I can't afford to violate truth and imperil my salvation for one duck." If it had been worth his while, he doubtless would have had no scruples, but he would not be drawn from the path of virtue and veracity without adequate inducement. I cannot help thinking that some of the agitators for the reduction of tithes must have a "one duck" conscience. With them it is a question of degree, not of principle. They say, in effect, that they would consider it wicked to pay £100 of tithe; but give them 20 per cent. reduction, and they will pay £80 without demur. And, unluckily, consciences of this kind have too often been treated with excessive tenderness. Clergymen have in a good many instances given reductions of tithe in cases where they had no business to do so. It is all very well to yield for the sake of peace and quietness, but I cannot help thinking that clergymen have done wrong in deferring to clamour in this matter. The incumbent ought to remember that he is the holder of a trust, and that if, during a succession of years, he accepts a sum less than that which the law gives him, he practically makes it impossible for his successor to obtain the income to which he is entitled, and in this way the property of the Church is permanently diminished. When he has received his tithes he is at perfect liberty to do what he likes with them, and he will naturally be ready to deal considerately with any individual cases of distress among the payers. But my point is that he ought to do this on personal, and not on general, grounds, and that if he consents to an all-round reduction, he transgresses the limits of justice.

On the other hand, I admit that the position is exceedingly difficult. Many a clergyman suffers much pecuniary inconvenience rather than take the odious step of distraining upon his parishioners, and most fair-minded men will be of opinion that this disagreeable alternative ought not to be forced upon him. Hitherto the cases of distraint have been extraordinarily few. Except in Wales, and in a few cases, such as those already mentioned, where the opposition has been prompted by purely political motives, there has, even in these hard times, been much less difficulty than one would have expected in obtaining payment. I am told by the manager of the Rent Guarantee Society, which is one of the largest agencies in the kingdom for collecting tithe rent-charge, that with proper tact on the part of the person who undertakes the work, there is very rarely any necessity to resort to legal measures. That society carries on its operations in most parts of the country, and it may fairly be inferred from its experience that the difficulties in Wales would not have arisen if it had not been for some personal hostilities and misunderstandings, which would probably have been obviated by the employment of such an agency for collection. Corporations, in Sydney Smith's phrase, have neither souls to be saved nor bodies to be kicked, and an organization of this kind, by its very impersonality, may save a clergyman from bitter and unseemly squabbles about money matters with his parishioners.

I cannot help thinking that the simplest solution of the difficulty would be to transfer the duty of collection from the clergy to the Ecclesiastical Commissioners. They are themselves the largest tithe-owners in existence, collecting no less than

£300,000 annually, or something like one-twelfth of the whole amount, from more than 50,000 tithe-payers in all parts of the kingdom. They therefore already possess the necessary machinery for the purpose; and this machinery would only want extension. That they would be ready to undertake the work may be inferred from the provision of Lord Salisbury's Tithe Bill (which received their approval) as to the compulsory redemption of small sums of tithe rent-charge. This provision (§ 11) would have empowered any incumbent or ecclesiastical corporation, entitled to tithe rent-charge of a less value than £2 a year, payable by a single owner, to require its redemption either by the payment of a capital sum equal to twenty-one years' purchase, or by payment to the Ecclesiastical Commissioners of an annuity for fifty-two years, calculated at the rate of £1 16*s*. for every £2 of the tithe rent-charge fixed by the apportionment. There is no doubt that the latter alternative would have been the one generally adopted. It would have meant, for example, that, in the present year, a rent-charge of the apportioned amount of 40*s*., but now represented, according to the tithe-averages, by the sum of 35*s*. 5*d*., would be redeemable by the annual payment of 36*s*. to the Commissioners until the year 1939. The difference would form a sinking fund for the redemption. The Commissioners would be responsible for the payment, in perpetuity, of the 35*s*. 5*d*. to the clerical tithe-owner, and for the collection of the 36*s*. from the tithe-payer. It is reasonable to suppose that at any rate all clergymen who experience the least difficulty in collecting small amounts of tithes would take advantage of this enactment. They would, indeed, if they were wise, lose no time in doing so, since the averages seem likely to get lower and lower, while the amount to be paid in redemption is fixed by the bill. Thus, if the averages descend to £75, a rent-charge of 40*s*. would be represented by 30*s*., but 36*s*. would, nevertheless, have to be paid for redemption. Although the bill was, of course, withdrawn last session, a measure on the subject is again promised, and we may assume that at any rate this clause will be retained.

If we consider the enormous number of tithe rent-charges that only amount to a few shillings apiece, it is clear that the provision in question would have soon thrown on the Commissioners the work of collecting a very large numerical proportion of the whole. (The fact that they would no longer be called tithe rent-charges, but annuities, is immaterial.) These small amounts are just those of which it is most difficult to obtain payment, and the Commissioners, being willing to undertake their collection, might just as well undertake the collection of the rest. The principle is, at any rate, established by the clause in question, and it is difficult to see why it should not be made generally applicable. If, as I believe to be the case, a trading company like the Rent Guarantee Society collects tithes, in ordinary circumstances, for a commission of $2\frac{1}{2}$ or 3 per cent., out of which they must make a profit, it ought to be possible for the Commissioners, with the nucleus of a collecting staff which they at present possess, to do the work on a large scale at a much smaller proportional cost. This cost, of (say) 1, or even 2 per cent., might of course be deducted in reimbursement of the Commissioners' expenses. Tithes are a first mortgage on the land, and there is no reason why their payment should not be enforced as rigidly as that of rates and taxes. The agent of the Commissioners might be armed with practically the same powers as the officers of the Inland Revenue; but even if the method of recovery were left as at present, the enforcement of payment by the department in Whitehall would be a very different matter from the claims of an individual clergyman.

Of course there are some difficulties in the way. In the first place, there is a widespread distrust, not altogether unfounded, of official administration; and, in the second place, objection may be raised—though, in my opinion, without substantial reason—to increasing the tax-collecting functions of the

Commissioners.[1] Moreover, though many clergymen would be only too glad to receive their tithes with the small deduction involved, others would grumble at it considerably. The rector of a parish in Lincolnshire told me that he had not the slightest difficulty in obtaining his tithes in full, and that the collection of £800 a year only cost £2 2s. for agency. There are, of course, the greatest differences between one district and another as regards both the cost of collection and the number of tithe-payers. Very often the whole tithe of a parish, sometimes of many parishes, is paid by a single landowner. On the other hand, I know of one parish in which there are more than a thousand tithe-payers, many of whom are only responsible for 2s. or 3s. apiece. The *Guardian* recently published a letter written to an official of the Church Defence Association in Wales by a clergyman whose tithe, of the nominal value of £138, is payable by 239 persons, in sums varying from 2d. to £3. Last year his net income was £74, and, contrary to general experience, though the poor people in the village paid every penny, the largest sum being 4s. 7d., the well-to-do farmers

---

[1] It should be remembered that the Ecclesiastical Commission is in no sense a government department, and that the salaries of the staff are not voted by Parliament, but are derived from Church funds. The change proposed would, therefore, give no colour to the suggestion that it would involve the payment of the clergy by the State.

are two years in arrear. If there is anything like organized hostility to the payment of tithe in a case of this kind, it is practically impossible for the clergyman to obtain his income. To distrain upon a couple of hundred parishioners would not be the best way of endearing himself to his flock, even if distraint, in respect of these small sums, were legally practicable.

There are two other points connected with tithe which may be dealt with, either together or separately, by legislation. The first is by whom it should be paid. The Act of 1836 provided distinctly that it should be payable by the landowner, and that every tenant who should thereafter pay it should be entitled to deduct the amount from the rent payable by him to his landlord; but the landlords have generally contracted themselves out of the obligation thus imposed upon them, and the ordinary practice has been to let land at a lower rent on condition that the tenant pays tithe as well as other outgoings. Lord Salisbury's bill of last session would in effect have prevented this course from being taken. It made the landlord exclusively responsible, and substituted for the process of distraint against the tenant that of the recovery of the amount from the landlord as a simple contract debt. No doubt it somewhat weakened the security, which at present is almost absolute. If the land is in cultivation, anything on it can now be distrained for tithe, and if it has been allowed to go to waste, distraint can be enforced for two years' arrears as soon as it is again farmed. There is something tangible to be laid hold of. On the other hand, the landlord may be embarrassed, living in Australia, or at Monte Carlo, and it may not be easy to get money from him. To meet this difficulty, it was proposed to give the County Court power to attach the rent by requiring the tenant to pay the tithe and deduct it from the amount due to his landlord. This provision would, I think, have removed all reasonable ground of objection, and there is no doubt that the Church at large accepted the measure with great favour as one that would have lessened a constant source of unpleasantness between parson and parishioners, though, of course, the debt would often have been only transferred from the farmer to the squire. Many landed proprietors already pay the tithes themselves, and in such cases the system works very smoothly. It is unfortunate that the Ecclesiastical Commissioners, who are very large tithe payers, do not follow this good example, for it is certainly anomalous that the chief authorities of the Church should be promoting legislation to make all landlords do on compulsion what they themselves fail to do voluntarily. This, however, is by the way.

It was at first proposed that the landowners should be allowed to deduct 5 per cent. from the tithe for the trouble of collecting it, but this was objected to as involving a transfer of something like £200,000 a year from the Church to the landowners. I confess that this figure appears to me to be much exaggerated. In the first place, of the total tithe rent-charge of £4,000,000, about two-fifths is in the hands of lay impropriators, and may be here left out of account. In the second place, at least 2 per cent. would be saved in cost of collection. In the third place, only a very sanguine person can anticipate that the value of tithe will be permanently above 80 per cent. The real loss, therefore, instead of being 5 per cent. on £4,000,000, would certainly not be more than 3 per cent. on £1,920,000, or £57,000; and if a sacrifice of this amount, which would be a little more than 6*d.* in the pound of tithe rent-charge, would solve the question of collection satisfactorily, the bargain would be a good one for the Church. However, the House of Lords struck the provision out of the bill, as giving an undue advantage to the landowners, and it is significant that while the Upper House, of which practically all the members are landed proprietors, performed what they considered to be an act of justice in this respect, and accepted the bill, though recognizing it to be to their own disadvantage, so much opposition to it was manifested in the Commons (partly, it is said, because the bribe of 5 per cent. was thus withdrawn) that the bill had to be dropped. It is to be hoped that in the interests not only of the Church, but of the settlement of an irritating question, it will be found possible to arrive at a satisfactory solution of the question next session. But I cannot help thinking that it would be wise only to deal with the tithes payable to parochial incumbents, and not with those belonging to lay impropriators. As Mr. Jasper More, M.P., very pertinently asked, in a letter which appeared in the *Morning Post* not long ago, why should one landowner, who has perhaps had to make large reductions in his rents, be forced to pay a brother landowner, who happens to be a lay impropriator, his income in full, while his own loss, if his tenants decline to pay the tithe to himself, will be crushing? If in any future measure this distinction between clerical and lay tithes were made, I fancy that much less opposition would be aroused in the House of Commons.

A second question, which has been much discussed lately, is the possibility of securing a general redemption of tithe. I confess that it seems to me doubtful whether the voluntary provisions of Lord Salisbury's bill as to this point would have been of much use. The capital sum to be paid for redemption was to be not less than twenty times the amount of the original appointment, and thus, taking the permanent value of the rent-charge at £80, it would cost at least £200 to redeem a payment of £8 a year. I do not imagine that this would have tempted many landowners, especially as capital is not too plentiful with them at the present time. No doubt the provision already described for the compulsory redemption of small amounts would have been serviceable. It would put a stop to the difficulty which now exists in some parishes, such as West Ham, where there are hundreds of tithe rent-charges amounting to only a few shillings each. The scheme of Mr. Ryde, President of the Institute of Surveyors, is more ambitious than Lord Salisbury's bill, and seems in some respects to offer special advantages. It was discussed in the *Quarterly Review* for July, 1886, and is exceedingly comprehensive. Whether it is sound from an actuarial point of view, and whether it would be practically workable, are questions into which I need not enter here.

There are two other points as to which I must say something before quitting the subject. The first is the question of revaluation. The farmers contend that the apportionment of 1836 was unfair to them, and that there ought to be a fresh valuation. To say nothing of the futility of attempting to reopen a question which was settled more than half a century ago, I think that the least inquiry would show that there is no hardship in the present arrangement. I have often heard it alleged that the commutation scheme was settled in the old times when the prices were high, and was therefore framed on an unfair basis. But, as a matter of fact, Mr. Whittle Harvey stated in the House of Commons, in 1836, that during the two preceding years agricultural produce had been unexampled in lowness of price. Agricultural distress had been referred to in the King's Speech, and a Royal Commission was appointed to report upon it. The average prices of the three grains—wheat, barley, and oats—on which the tithe averages are calculated, were actually less in 1835 than in 1883. Moreover, as I have pointed out, the tithe had been taken not only on grain, but on other farm produce—hay, cattle, sheep, eggs, and milk—the value of which has enormously increased in the last fifty years. Whether some change might not fairly be made in the period upon which the averages are calculated is another question. Under the present plan of seven years' averages it may happen that the highest tithe has to be paid when prices are lowest, and *vice versâ*. For instance, the averages in 1854 were £91, though the prices of that particular year would have been represented by £123, while, on the other hand, the averages for 1887 are £88, though present prices would only represent about £69. It may happen, therefore, that when the farmer is getting high prices he has to pay less in tithes, and when he is getting low prices he has to pay more. Still, of course, any shortening of the term of averages at the present moment would temporarily be very disadvantageous to the clergy.

As regards the rating of tithe rent-charge, I cannot help thinking that the incumbents are rather hardly treated. Their income from tithe is in the nature of a fixed stipend for the performance of certain specified duties, and they complain that it is subject to local burdens from which allowances from the Ecclesiastical Commissioners are exempt. I know of a case, by no means an exceptional one, in which the entire rateable value of a parish is £2093, while the rateable value of the tithe rent-charge, as settled by the Assessment Committee, is no less than £405. Here, then, the rector has to pay on his tithe alone, without taking into account the rectory and glebe, about a fifth of the rates of the whole parish, whereas it would seem fair that he should at any rate not pay more than a tenth. The result is, that rates absorb as nearly as possible a quarter of the income of the living. A short time ago, an instance of the same kind, though scarcely of the same degree, of hardship was given in the *Morning Post* by the Rev. W. Burleigh, and the point certainly deserves consideration in the readjustment of local taxation which is promised by Mr. Goschen. When the question was raised on the discussion of the Commutation Bill in the House of Commons in 1836,

Lord John Russell said that "many of the rates are now diminishing, and it would be difficult to make a deduction on account of them." When commutations were based on past agreements to pay an annual sum free of rates, an addition was made equivalent to the estimated amount. This being the case, it is not to be expected that the rent-charge should be exempted from the numerous local burdens of the present day; but it would perhaps be reasonable that a limitation should be introduced, so that the assessment of tithe should not exceed one-tenth of that of the parish from which it is derived. Such a provision would afford some relief to a class of the clergy who now, in various ways, have to pay much more than their fair share of every kind of local contribution, whether voluntary in name or obligatory in law.

CHAPTER IX.

CHARGES ON LIVINGS.

"DILAPIDATIONS, pensions to retired incumbents, payments to Queen Anne's Bounty." These are words which have been unpleasantly dinned into my ears in the course of my inquiries among the rural clergy, all of whom seem to have a grievance under one head or the other; and when a gentleman in the country has a real *bête noire*, it is sure to crop up in his conversation as persistently as Charles I.'s head in Mr. Dick's memorial. It may be well, therefore, for me to discuss these subjects before I sum up the general results of my investigations. As to dilapidations, I need say little. It seems to be quite reasonable that each incumbent should, so to speak, hold his house and other buildings upon a repairing lease, and that he or his executors should be pecuniarily responsible for handing over the property in a good condition to his successor. Any other arrangement would be sure to result in parsonages and barns going to rack and ruin. It is true that here and there an impoverished incumbent who has spent nothing on repairs is prevented from resigning his living, even to take a better one, by the amount which he would have to pay for dilapidations. But this is his own fault or misfortune, as the case may be, and the only substantial ground of complaint in connection with this matter seems to be that some of the fees payable to diocesan officials are still unreasonably high, though I believe that they have been lowered of late years.

The pensions granted to retired incumbents have in many cases proved a terrible burden on benefices largely affected by the agricultural depression. This is what has happened over and over again :—The rector of a living which ten years ago was worth £600 a year, derived from the rent of glebe, retired at that time on a pension of £200 a year. The act allows one-third of the net income to be granted as pension, and in most cases that maximum has been given. What is the result now? Of course, the late incumbent, like most annuitants, gets so much into the habit of living that he cannot break himself of it; he seems to have a fair prospect of surviving to be a centenarian; and his pension has to be paid regularly. But the glebe of 300 acres, which fetched £600 in 1877, only with difficulty realizes £300 in 1887, and the result is that there is a balance of just £100 a year left for the actual rector, who does all the work, and on whom falls the burden of most of the parochial charities.

I am glad to say that such injustice will be to some extent remedied for the future. A bill on the subject, which was safely piloted through Parliament last session, and the meritorious character of which seems to have disarmed even the hostility of the Irish members, has now become law, and provides that all future pensions, where the income of the living is derived from tithe rent-charge or from glebe, shall be regulated by the tithe averages, so that at the present time, when tithe is twelve below par, a pension of £100 would be represented by £88, and if, as is anticipated, those averages go down to £75, that sum only would be paid. Moreover, in the grant of a pension a sufficient income is to be left to provide for the due performance of the services of the Church according to the statutory scale of stipends. These provisions will go some way towards preventing what in many instances has been gross unfairness, although they will, of course, not adequately meet those cases where the reduction of income arises from the fact that a large proportion of the glebe, though let when the pension was granted, becomes tenantless afterwards. On the other hand, where a pension is given while things are at their lowest, the rector who follows may subsequently prove a gainer by the new basis of calculation ; and I am inclined to think that the plan of revaluation every five years, as proposed by the committee of Convocation, would have been fairer to both parties. Still, the new Act is a great improvement on the old one, and its promoters deserve great credit for having managed to get it passed in a session when legislation of all kinds was unprecedentedly difficult.

Queen Anne's Bounty Office is among the most abused of public departments. No doubt one reason for this is that a man always detests his creditors, and that a very large proportion of the clergy find it irksome to have to make periodical payments, often in respect of debts which their predecessors have contracted, to the governors of the fund. But it will be naturally asked, "What sort of 'bounty' is that which exacts payment from the clergy, instead of helping them, and how is it that at the present time the charges levied by the Bounty Office are among those which press most hardly on incumbents?" The explanation is that the governors of Queen Anne's Bounty have not only to administer charity, but to conduct a gigantic mortgage business. Two committees of Convocation, to say nothing of a Select Committee of the House of Commons, have investigated the working of the system, and their reports throw a good deal of light on a subject as to which there has been much misapprehension. It seems that the original fund administered by the Bounty

Board was founded in 1704, when Queen Anne, at the instance of Bishop Burnet, devoted to the purpose of "augmenting the incomes of the poorer clergy," the "firstfruits and tenths" which had been payable to the Crown from chapters and benefices, and which amount altogether to between £13,000 and £15,000 a year. The fund was placed under the management of a board, consisting of the archbishops, bishops, deans, the Speaker, all Privy Councillors, lords lieutenant, judges, Queen's Counsel, mayors of cities, officers of the Board of Green Cloth, and clerks of the Privy Council, the total number being something like 600. It need scarcely be said that few of these exalted functionaries take any part in the work; and I have some doubt as to whether an average Q.C. or provincial mayor is even aware of the fact that he is a member of the board. I understand that the bishops attend by rota, that the Duke of Buckingham and Chandos is the most active of the laymen who now take part in the business, and that Lord Beauchamp, Mr. Cubitt, and Mr. Calvert, Q.C., are also prominent members. The operations of the governors are thus described in the report presented to Convocation this year by a committee, of which the Bishops of London and Hereford were members :—

"The Bounty Office has a double function to discharge. The primary duty of the governors is to apply to the augmentation of small livings the income derived from firstfruits and tenths paid by the holders of certain benefices. This income amounts to about £13,000 a year, grants from which are always made either for the improvement of parsonage houses or of small livings, or (far more commonly) to increase their permanent endowments, by meeting benefactions given for the same purposes. The usual grant is £200 to meet a benefaction of £200. The £400 thus obtained is in some cases invested in land, which thenceforward becomes part of the freehold of the holder of the benefice. But it is frequently retained by the governors, and invested in their name, in securities of various kinds, the governors undertaking to pay the holder of the benefice interest on the money so invested. The amount thus retained by the governors is now very considerable, but it is obvious that it is trust-money, held in trust for the clergy who hold the augmented benefices. Among the various modes in which the governors are allowed to invest this trust capital, they are empowered to lend it to the clergy on the security of their benefices for repairs and improvements of various kinds; and this investment of a portion of this trust capital is a very important part of their business. It will be seen from this statement that the Bounty Office is first a grant-office, and secondly a loan-office. As a grant-office, it administers a charity, and looks mainly to the poverty of the living which it is asked to augment. As a loan-office, its primary duty is to see that, in lending trust-money (which is in reality the property of the poorer clergy, for only small livings are augmented), full security is obtained for the replacement of the capital and the punctual payment of the interest. To allow the capital to be lost is to rob the benefices; to allow the interest to be lost is to rob the present holders. The applicants to the Bounty Office for loans seem often not to be aware of the double function of the office, and expect to get loans on easier terms, as if in making these loans the governors were dealing, not with trust property belonging to the poorer clergy, but with some fund placed at their disposal for the purpose of facilitating improvements and repairs of the property of all the clergy alike. But the governors are never at liberty to forget whose money it is, and have no right to imperil it. The clergy may always borrow elsewhere, and give precisely the same security, and may thus have recourse to any lender, if they can find one who is willing to lend on easier terms; but, having some considerable acquaintance with the business of the board, we are of opinion that the governors cannot lend at a lower rate than at present without in some degree endangering the absolute safety of the money which they hold in trust, and of the annual payments which they are bound to make to the holders of the augmented benefices."

This report furnishes a satisfactory answer to the objection that the Bounty Office conducts its business on commercial and not on charitable principles. It is no doubt a great convenience to an incumbent, when a parsonage has to be rebuilt, or when money is required for farm buildings or the repair of a chancel, to be able to obtain a loan for the purpose on fair terms; and it cannot be said that 4 per cent. interest is an excessively high rate, or that 20 or 30 years is an unreasonable period for repayment. Incoming rectors, too, who have found themselves saddled with a large expenditure for dilapidations due to the default of their predecessors, have often been relieved from much difficulty by having recourse to the Bounty Office. But where the parson's income has been diminished by 40 or 50 per cent. since the loan was effected, the annual charge has become a very serious burden. I have met with one case, for example, in which the sum of £2000 was borrowed in respect of a large glebe when it produced a rental of between £800 and £900 a year. The rental has now sunk to about £400; and the £130 which the incumbent paid last year to the governors of Queen Anne's Bounty actually exceeded his own net income after payment of rates, taxes, and other necessary outgoings.

It is to meet such cases that the governors have recently obtained parliamentary powers enabling them, "when the income of a benefice has been materially diminished by the reduction in letting value of any glebe land," to extend the term for repayment of loans ; and early in the present year they issued a circular to nearly 2000 incumbents, expressing their willingness to consider applications for the exercise of such powers. About one-third of this number applied, and up to the middle of August an extension had been granted in 144 cases, the effect being, as regards most of them, to diminish the annual instalment of principal by about one-half. The governors had previously, under a temporary Act of 1881, suspended for one, two, or three years the instalments due in 335 cases, and they seem therefore to have acted with the utmost consideration for the pecuniary difficulties of their mortgagees. But in this matter they are, as I have already remarked, exercising the functions of trustees, and they have no authority to remit any part of the loans.

As a matter of fact, the bad debts of the governors of Queen Anne's Bounty are very few, though they very rarely have to resort to legal proceedings to enforce payment. They have a capital of rather over £1,000,000 outstanding on about 4000 mortgages of benefices ; but the arrears of more than one year's standing amount to less than £3000. They may certainly be charged with having in former times allowed unnecessarily large parsonages to be built, sometimes with an amount of stabling more suited to a trainer of racehorses than to a country rector with £200 or £400 a year. But under the existing administration, which has undergone many changes for the better since the appointment of Mr. J. K. Aston as secretary and treasurer, overbuilding has been discouraged, and the present practice of taking all possible precautions to secure substantial erections, so that fresh loans may not be required for repairs, is dictated by common sense. The governors hold Church funds amounting altogether to about £4,600,000, and last year their payments in augmentation of poor livings were nearly £140,000. On the whole, therefore, I cannot avoid the conclusion that their action has done and is doing much to lessen the hardships which have befallen the clergy in consequence of the agricultural depression, and that they cannot fairly be blamed for having granted loans for drainage and farm buildings at a time when there was every reason to believe that the expenditure would be productive, although the result has no doubt in many cases been the imposition of serious burdens on the now reduced incomes. But if, as has been suggested, the rate of interest were reduced from 4 to 3 per cent., the mortgagees would be benefited at the expense of the Bounty fund, and this would be unfair. Anomalous as is the constitution of the board of governors, their work seems to be efficient, and their investments, which are not restricted to government securities, to have been judiciously selected. There is, perhaps, some danger that Church funds of nearly five millions sterling, in the hands of one body, may hereafter prove a tempting bait to the advocates of Disestablishment. Fortunately, however, this danger is at present remote.

CHAPTER X.

RECAPITULATION.

IN this final chapter I purpose to summarize the results of my inquiries as to the effect of the agricultural depression upon the incomes of the clergy, to make some suggestions as to legislation, and to give some account of what is being done to relieve the more acute cases of distress which have lately arisen. In the first place, it seems clear that the greatest loss of clerical income has been in the Midlands, where it is mainly dependent on glebe, and the least in some of the grazing counties, such as Devonshire, where it chiefly arises from tithe rent-charge, and where the farmers, though by no means flourishing, have not been reduced to such a desperate condition as to make the collection of tithe a difficulty. As far as agriculture alone is concerned, I am inclined to think that Essex has suffered more than any other county, as it contains at the present moment many thousand acres of land which used to yield some of the finest wheat crops in England, but which are now absolutely uncultivated. The Ecclesiastical Commissioners have farms there of an aggregate extent of 4000 or 5000 acres which they are unable to let, and are forced to cultivate by the agency of bailiffs, probably at a loss. There is plenty of land in the immediate neighbourhood of Chelmsford, itself one of the best corn markets in the kingdom, which cost £60 an acre ten years ago, and which is now offered for sale at £10 without attracting a purchaser. Even a small farm of between 50 and 60 acres in the same neighbourhood, which used to be worth at least £50 an acre, was recently put up to auction, and failed to realize the reserve price of £8 an acre, although holdings of this size are still generally much more saleable than larger ones. Another Essex farm, bought at £2500, has just fetched £800. Even market-garden land at Ilford, within eight miles of London, which was formerly let at £3 10s. an acre, now only fetches 30s., the depreciation being mainly due to the foreign competition in vegetables, although partly, perhaps, to the fact that the fumes from the numerous chemical works on the eastern outskirts of the metropolis are believed to be exercising an injurious effect upon vegetation. On the whole, however, though the condition of agriculture in the stiff clays of Essex is almost without parallel, the clergy have not suffered to a corresponding extent, owing to the fact that the amount of glebe is relatively insignificant. In fact, there are only four livings with as much as 200 acres attached to them, and only about twenty others with even half that amount. Still I have heard of two cases in Essex, in each of which the glebe of about 100 acres has gone out of cultivation for lack of tenants; and it may be said that although the average amount of glebe is small, its former value has ordinarily decreased by about 40 per cent. It is, however, in the Midlands, where, as a general rule, the incumbents depend almost entirely upon glebe, that the greatest hardship had arisen. I have given particulars of many cases where the emoluments of the benefice have been brought down so low as scarcely to leave a bare maintenance for the parson after the payment of necessary outgoings. Without repeating details, I shall convey some idea of the extent of the losses of the clergy by saying that forty livings in the dioceses of Peterborough and Ely, which are practically solely dependent on glebe, averaging 270 acres apiece, were ten years ago of the mean value of £494 each, and are now worth just over £180. When we consider that from this reduced income have to be deducted outgoings of various kinds; that charities and parochial institutions have to be kept up; that there are often heavy charges for repayments to Queen Anne's Bounty or to land improvement societies, and sometimes pensions to retired incumbents—it is not to be wondered at that many rectors and vicars are now struggling with the direst necessity.

Incumbents mainly paid from tithe rent-charge are much better off. It is true that their income is already 12 per cent. below par, and something like 25 per cent. below the inflated averages of ten years ago. But, as a general rule, the tithe has been paid, though often not without much delay, and in some of the districts where the farmers have been hardest hit, not without substantial reduction. Of organized opposition there appears at present to be little, though it is to be feared that a quasi-political agitation on the subject is smouldering in a good many places, and that it may burst forth if, in the long run, the Welsh farmers are allowed to be victorious in the struggle which they have begun. It has been noticed that the movement is mainly fostered by men who have recently bought their land very cheaply, and who are attempting to enhance its value in this illegitimate fashion. It seems certain that the tithe averages, being based on the price of corn, will continue to fall steadily for some years to come; and it is anticipated by experts that the permanent value of £100 of tithe rent-charge in this country is eventually likely to be something between £70 and £75. This will mean a loss of not far short of £700,000 annually to the Church in the income of beneficed incumbents alone, to say nothing of those chapters and other ecclesiastical corporations which are tithe-owners. Yet, despite agricultural depression, the land rental of the whole of England, urban and rural together, is steadily rising, and it is a serious thing that, with an increasing population, the ancient endowments of the Church should undergo this diminution. It is true that any squire whose property is exclusively in agricultural land suffers with the parson, but the squire is free to engage in what pursuits he chooses and to live where he likes; whereas the parson is compelled by law to perform certain defined duties, is prohibited from engaging in secular pursuits, is tied to his own parish, and is practically obliged to supply not only the religious, but many of the material wants of his parishioners.

I am afraid that so far as the glebe owner is concerned, legislation will afford very little help. Two Acts of the past session have been already mentioned, the first enabling the Governors of Queen Anne's Bounty to extend the time, and therefore lessen the instalments, for the repayment of loans granted for the erection of parsonage houses and farm buildings, and the drainage of land; the second providing that in future the pensions of retiring incumbents shall not be of constant amount, but shall vary with the tithe averages. These two measures will afford some slight relief in many cases; and a third, which was unluckily blocked last session, would have removed some disabilities and some injustice under which the clerical glebe-owner labours when, in default of a tenant, he has to cultivate his own land. But the law cannot do much more than this for him. His income is bound up with the prosperity of agriculture, and, as agriculture decays, his income must dwindle, perhaps even to the vanishing point.

The case of the tithe-owner is different. There seems to be a tolerably universal agreement among friends of the Church that the present mode of collection requires amendment, tending, as it does, to interfere with the proper relations between parson and parishioners. The ordinary remedy suggested is merely to apply universally the principle embodied in the 80th section of the Tithe Commutation Act, to the effect that the rent-charge should be payable by the landlord, not by the tenant. In introducing that measure, Lord John Russell said that "the income of the clergy will now flow from the landowners, and not from each tenant or farmer, and the clergy will be relieved from the alternative which now too often exists, either of making personal enemies by pressing their demands, or injuring themselves by abandoning them." But a large proportion of the landowners have contracted themselves out of this obligation by bargaining that their tenants should pay the tithes as well as all other outgoings. Lord Salisbury's bill would have prohibited this arrangement, and, by making the landowner in all cases directly responsible, would have undoubtedly gone some way towards a solution of the problem. But would it have gone far enough? There is a prevalent notion that the persons who own land chargeable with the tithe are comparatively few in number, while those who rent land, and merely pay on their landlord's behalf, in accordance with a clause in their lease, are very numerous. This notion is, I think, an exaggerated one. There is, unfortunately, no complete return of the number of tithe-payers in England, though one would have thought that exact information on this point was a necessary preliminary to legislation on the subject. But the Ecclesiastical Commissioners derive an income of about £300,000 a year from tithe rent-charge, and they have recently obtained statistics as to the persons liable for this amount. They find that it comes from land owned by 37,000 landlords, and occupied by 55,000 tenants; and that it is mostly, but not universally, paid by the latter. Supposing that the tenants who pay are 50,000, the transfer of the obligation to the landlord would only reduce the payments from that number to 37,000, and it is a question whether it is worth while to take much trouble for the sake of so small a saving. If the same proportion obtains throughout the tithe rent-charges of the country, the transfer would diminish the number of payers by only 26 per cent. Lord

Addington mentioned, at the recent Oxford Diocesan Conference, that in a single Welsh parish there were no less than 300 tithe-payers who were also owners, and in such an instance the provisions of Lord Salisbury's bill would have been of little avail, except as regards the compulsory redemption of rent-charges under £2.

But the clause on this latter subject would have practically enabled any incumbent to transfer to the Ecclesiastical Commissioners the duty of collecting the annuity representing tithes of small amount, and, for the reasons given in a previous chapter, I cannot help thinking that this duty might well be extended to the Commissioners in respect of all existing tithe rent-charges. This alteration would make it of much less importance whether the tithe were paid by the landlord or by the tenant. The collector of tithes on behalf of the Commissioners might be practically placed in much the same position as the collector of taxes on behalf of the Inland Revenue ; indeed, the same person might be employed. The clergyman would no longer be in the invidious position of having to distrain upon his parishioners, and the payment would be in a great degree divested of its special character. The charge would be paid with the rates and taxes, and would before long come to be regarded in the same light as those imposts—as unpleasant but inevitable. The recalcitrant landlord or tenant, no matter which, who would not hesitate to press a poor parson for abatement or exemption, would find some difficulty in withstanding a body like the Ecclesiastical Commissioners, whose duty it would be to collect the amount inexorably, and to pay it over to the incumbent. It would, on the other hand, be entirely for the latter to decide whether, having received the money, he should make an allowance to such of the tithe-payers as might be in need of special consideration. With respect to the often excessive rating of tithe, I have already pointed out the importance of dealing with the question in any new scheme of local taxation, and I need not repeat what I have said on the subject.

With regard to the best means of meeting the distress which is steadily becoming more widespread among the clergy, and which is likely to be much increased in the present winter, it seems very desirable that help should be afforded by the Ecclesiastical Commissioners where the income has fallen so low as not to provide a bare maintenance for the clergymen of parishes with more than a certain number of inhabitants. There are some livings at the present time for which it is impossible to obtain incumbents, and the parishioners are left without the ministrations of religion because nobody can be found to take a benefice of which the outgoings exceed the receipts. There ought to be some relaxation of the rule which restricts the Commissioners to the grant of permanent endowments. They should be empowered to afford temporary aid in special circumstances, so as, at any rate, to provide a certain small minimum for the maintenance of an incumbent in cases where the income of a living has been swept away by the impossibility of letting glebe. But, of course, one difficulty is that the Commissioners, as very large landowners, have themselves suffered to a large extent. Their able financial secretary, Mr. Porter, in his very practical evidence before Mr. Bridge in connection with the Welsh tithe riots, explained that the income of the Commissioners during the last few years had been reduced by over £100,000 a year, and the result is that the funds at their disposal for new grants are comparatively small.

It is perhaps desirable to point out, however, that about a quarter of this amount represents the difference between the proceeds of the episcopal estates which they manage and the sums which they have to pay to the bishops in respect of those estates. If the property of a cathedral chapter falls in value, nobody suffers but the dean and canons, who find their incomes diminished. But with episcopal endowments the case is different. If a bishop finds his estates producing less, in bad times, than his normal income, though in good times they may have given him a large surplus, he is entitled to transfer them to the Commissioners, who have to make good any deficiency of revenue. Last year, their payments for this purpose were over £25,000, and of course the sum available for the augmentation of poor livings was diminished by just this amount. I am well aware that bishops have large claims upon them, and that in very many cases, though not in all, most of their income is spent upon Church objects. But the drain upon funds of the Commissioners, which might more properly be devoted to the relief of the parochial clergy, is a very serious one; and I hope that it will not be considered a very Radical proposal if I suggest that, in the case of all future episcopal appointments, the nominal incomes should follow the tithe averages, so that, for instance, during the present year each £100 should be only worth £87 8s. 10d. As the total income of the Episcopal bench amounts to £170,000 a year, this arrangement would release, for the augmentation of poor livings, about £21,000, or £4000 less than has been diverted from that object in the fashion which I have indicated.[1]

For the immediate relief of urgent cases of distress among the clergy, there are in London two

---

[1] The principle of regulating, by the tithe averages, an income not necessarily derived from tithe, is established by the Act of last session, already referred to, with reference to the pensions of superannuated incumbents.

charitable societies of importance. One of these, the Poor Clergy Relief Corporation, habitually expends over £7000 a year in grants to the poorer clergy, their widows and orphans, and appeals for assistance have never been so numerous as at present—indeed, many clergymen who have been subscribers in former years have now been compelled to apply for help. The grants of this body, however, only average about £10, and never exceed £25, and doles of this amount, however acceptable to a person reduced to destitution, are obviously inadequate to meet the present emergency. The other society is the Corporation of the Sons of the Clergy, which for more than two centuries has carried on its beneficent work of assisting necessitous clergymen, pensioning their widows, and educating, apprenticing, and providing outfits for their children, and which expends on these objects something like £24,000 a year. The charity is administered with great care and efficiency, and it occurred to the Archbishop of Canterbury that a special fund might be raised to deal temporarily with individual cases of distress directly arising out of the present agricultural depression, and that the experience of the society might be made available for its distribution. So an appeal was made to the public in February last, and up to the present time about £38,000, including a donation of £200 from the Queen, have been subscribed.

This Clergy Distress Fund [1] is devoted to the temporary assistance of beneficed clergymen now under pecuniary pressure due to (1) reduction of rent of glebe, (2) losses from farming glebe for which no tenant can be found, (3) non-payment of tithe, (4) inability to pay loans advanced on glebe, and (5) difficulty in keeping up premiums of insurance. The utmost care is taken to ascertain the urgency of the need; each application must be vouched for and recommended by the archdeacon and by the bishop of the diocese, and must contain particulars of all income due, and of all income received in the past twelve months, of the number of children dependent or partly dependent upon the applicant of all charges on the benefices, rates and taxes, insurance premiums, and subscriptions. It has been the aim of the society to give substantial aid likely to be of lasting benefit, and many of the grants have been of considerable amount. The total number has been about 170, and the sum already expended has been rather over £16,000. The average amount granted has thus been nearly £100, but in some cases it has been as little as £25, while six of the applicants who have suffered most have had £250

[1] Any of my readers who may desire to obtain further information on the subject, or to contribute to the Clergy Distress Fund, should communicate with Mr. W. Paget Bowman, registrar to the Corporation of the Sons of the Clergy, 2, Bloomsbury Place.

apiece. In one of the latter cases I have reason to believe that it was the grant alone which saved the glebe from being sold under the powers of a special Act of the land improvement company which had advanced money upon it. It is feared that the distress among the clergy will be intensified this winter, and demands upon the fund will pour in during the next few months to an extent which it will be difficult to satisfy, unless large contributions are received. It is a work in which all Churchmen may well be asked to join, and it is much to be desired that collections on its behalf should be made in all churches. I have said enough to show the extremity of the need, and the practical certainty that the hardships of the clergy will, at least for some time, continue to increase.

Perhaps I may venture to hope that the facts which I have brought together may convince my readers of the necessity for vigorous and comprehensive action in a matter affecting the welfare both of parsons and parishioners, and that I may at least be thought to have indicated one or two simple remedies for some formidable ills.

APPENDIX A.

The following letter appeared in the *Morning Post* of November 2, 1887 :—

Sir,—Your Special Commissioner's articles have admirably stated the case. I give you now my own experience as a country rector for the past twelve months. A year ago, all my glebe, over 400 acres, was unlet. I was obliged to employ an agent, whose services, including advertisements, have cost me £35. I have received about £200 in rents. Out of this sum I have to pay £230 for a rent-charge on the glebe, over £20 for land tax, tenths amounting to £2 7s. to Queen Anne's Bounty, and I know not what else. The benefice was, a few years ago, worth over £600 a year net. Now its value, as you see, is represented by a *minus* quantity. But what can I do? I cannot obtain a curacy, as some objection to my family of seven children, or that I am too old, having been in orders twenty years, is sure to prove a bar. All my insurance policies have had to be surrendered to have something to be going on with, in the hope that better times were coming. My table has been innocent of a joint of meat for the last two months, our dinners at the most being made up from the garden produce, with an occasional slice of bacon. Skim milk we get certainly at a small price—a penny a quart—and have plenty of puddings, rice, sago, etc. Of course we don't starve. As for fuel, we are chiefly dependent on wood. Clothes come from relatives; but several of these are much in the same plight as ourselves. I could name several others in a like position, where *res angustæ domi* necessitate the very strictest economy, even to the watering down of ink and using half a sheet of paper on which to write a polite note. All the time we are not unemployed, but at work from 7 a.m. to 9.30 p.m. I doubt not that what I have written will seem incredible to many, but it is only a very small description of what many are now undergoing. The purchase of a new book, or even a magazine, is never thought of. Now and then some book is borrowed, and eagerly read. The Church papers are never seen. It is, indeed, a matter of working for love. I enclose my card, for I have some left from better times, and subscribe myself, for I wish no one but yourself to know, who is a

COUNTRY RECTOR.

October 31.

APPENDIX B.

TABLE SHOWING AREA AND VALUE OF GLEBE LAND.

Diocese.	Total No. of Benefices.	Area of Glebe.	Gross Estimated Rental.	Average Glebe per Living.
		Acres.	£	Acres.
Bangor	139	4,292	3,388	31
Bath and Wells	492	16,648	29,626	34
Canterbury	434	4,749	8,168	11
Carlisle	292	24,268	24,124	83
Chester	267	3,737	8,184	14
Chichester	392	6,928	11,180	18
Durham	238	8,661	10,289	36
Ely	559	49,396	57,911	88
Exeter	519	22,658	30,752	43
Gloucester and Bristol	490	30,370	36,671	62
Hereford	385	15,068	19,168	39
Lichfield	460	12,201	21,559	26
Lincoln	586	67,818	87,132	116
Liverpool	193	2,401	5,643	13
Llandaff	236	8,081	11,987	34
London	542	4,922	24,851	9
Manchester	503	8,059	22,619	16
Newcastle	156	5,641	7,632	36
Norwich	897	28,416	37,481	32
Oxford	647	44,720	56,862	69
Peterborough	580	74,633	107,661	129
Ripon	503	22,445	28,825	45
Rochester	321	1,730	7,827	5
St. Albans	605	18,756	23,864	31
St. Asaph	206	4,655	5,310	22
St. David's	400	24,561	18,383	61
Salisbury	483	17,693	24,171	37
Sodor and Man	35	498	752	14
Southwell	470	32,747	48,589	69
Truro	237	8,313	11,604	35
Winchester	559	9,986	13,334	18
Worcester	396	28,850	45,156	73
York	627	45,647	57,579	73
	13,849	659,548	£908,282	48

www.ingramcontent.com/pod-product-compliance
Lightning Source LLC
Chambersburg PA
CBHW021941160426
43195CB00011B/1180